MW01113965

...000.733.8729 or
visit us at www.choicesforparents.org.

AMERICA'S SIMPLE SOLUTIONS

A VISIONARY'S BLUEPRINT
FOR A BETTER TOMORROW

MARK WERTS

COOL
TITLES

Published by
Cool Titles
439 N. Canon Dr., Suite 200
Beverly Hills, CA 90210
www.cooltitles.com

The Library of Congress Cataloging-in-Publication Data Applied For

Mark Werts—
America's Simple Solutions: A Visionary's Blueprint for a Better Tomorrow

p.   cm
ISBN 978-1-935270-41-6
1. Political Science/Political Freedom 2. Political Science/Political Economy
3. Political Science/Commentary and Opinion
I. Title
2016

Printed in the United States of America

3 5 7 9 10 8 6 4 2

Book editing and design by White Horse Enterprises, Inc.

For interviews or information regarding special discounts for bulk purchases,
please contact cindy@cooltitles.com

Distributed by Midpoint Trade

***Disclaimer: All quotes are written "as is," and no changes have been
made to correct grammar or punctuation.**

Dedication

To my five kids and two grandkids: Julian, Zoey, MW Jr., Iggy and Chloe, Ekena and Adora, that they might know increasing personal freedoms.

Table of Contents

Introduction

DURING MANY POINTS IN TIME IN OUR world's past, one lone person has made a monumental and historical decision. That decision changed the course of history, the course of a nation, and the lives and future of many people. We can open history books from almost any time or any culture and identify these important decisions and events that were set in motion by the strength, courage, and vision of one human being.

Several of these moments stand out in my mind. Twenty odd years ago in Africa, a prisoner who had been jailed for twenty-six years had his jail door opened by his guard. The prisoner was free to go, but he refused to leave his cell until all of his people were freed. Because of Nelson Mandela's decision, a new and just rainbow nation was reborn in the Southern Hemisphere.

Our own American history is also full of such momentous events. When a group of colonial renegades had enough of their colonial masters, they threw the contents of a trading vessel packed with tea into Boston Harbor. With their demand of "no taxation without representation," those few outlaws sparked a war that brought about the birth of our new American nation. Later in this new nation, there was a convention of visionary men of various backgrounds, beliefs, faiths, economical circumstance, and political slant. Together they drew up a document that outlined the new rules of the game. This Bill of Rights pointed the way toward the future of the new nation, and became a game plan for how things should evolve.

We have had many men (and women) who were thrust onto the scene by the vote of the people, leaders who were elected into positions of power. These people courageously made singular and far reaching decisions that changed history. Abraham Lincoln was one such man. Franklin Delano Roosevelt was another. In the 1930s Roosevelt implemented "temporary" measures that re-instilled confidence in a country that was blighted by economic depression. Temporary measures, although some of them are still in place today. He also took up the fight for a renewal of freedom and democracy, which by 1941 had been reduced to a mere eleven countries.

Those countries were, in alphabetical order, Australia, Canada, Chile, Finland, Iceland, Ireland, New Zealand, Sweden, Switzerland, United Kingdom, and the United States. You can read more about this in *The Third Wave: Democratization in the Late Twentieth Century* by Samuel P. Huntington.

Certainly, John F. Kennedy's decision about missiles placed in Cuba by our adversaries at the time, the Russians, was a momentous event. So was Ronald Reagan's single-handed face down of Soviet leader Mikhail Gorbachev. That brought about the fall of the Berlin Wall, and ended both the Cold War and the insane race that counted how many times we could annihilate mankind. We also have to remember Reagan's equally courageous face down of the tax and spend 1980 American Congress. That was a group who refused to curtail their spending ways, in spite of the destructive course of economic realities it had brought about, including 22 percent interest rates.

We Americans are again at a monumental juncture, and the future of individual freedom and democracy is at stake. Today we are faced with decisions that could re-ignite the unbelievable success our experiment in democracy has been over the last two hundred plus years. That re-ignition, however, will only happen if we find Americans with a global vision to step forward, take a position, and make hard decisions.

These Americans must be leaders from the ground up. From our local school boards, mayors, and county commissioners all the way up to our national leaders, our elected men and women must be able to see the big picture, and how we Americans, our townships, cities, and states all fit into this new, global view.

If we can't find those people we will continue on our current journey, a journey that allows us to forget the ideas and values that made America great. If that happens, America will become one more experiment that had its time. We will be remembered as a country that couldn't adapt to a changing global world, the changing geographic economic balance, or the many emerging and newly powerful nations. We will become a country that couldn't learn from its own failures or the failures of others around the globe. We will have been a country that lost focus, condemned like an aging athlete to exit the spotlight. Americans will then be the audience that watches a new global drama unfold with a new set of players.

Our elected men and women must be able to see the big picture, and how we Americans, our townships, cities, and states all fit into this new, global view.

Fortunately, this scenario is not inevitable. Those visionary guys in Philadelphia in 1776 prepared us for the possibility of all of these events unfolding, and gave us all the tools we need to halt the decline, wise up, and set in motion a rebirth and continuation of our historic success. It will be up to us, though, to find our new visionaries, put them into positions and clean up our well-intentioned mistakes.

The following chapters will cover many of the issues that Americans face today. Common sense solutions will be also discussed, solutions that can advance individual freedom and democracy, and jump-start our entrepreneurial creativity and historic American economic success. These solutions might even create a new well-being for our entire society, and America could once again become the shining light, beacon of hope, and leading example of success in this new global environment.

Like you, I have a lot of ideas about what went wrong in America and how we can fix it. But unlike you, perhaps, I am a global businessman. For more than forty years I have lived or done business in Italy, England, the Netherlands, Switzerland, Spain, France, Hong Kong, Japan, Turkey, North Africa, South Africa, Southeast Asia, and China, as well as America. Most of my businesses have been in the world of fashion, and I am the founder of a store called American Rag, Cie. It is a unique, specialty-clothing store, with numerous locations around the world. My global perspective is definitely up close and personal, rather than theoretical.

I have no political party affiliation, and no agenda. And, I am not running for any office. Simply put, I see that our country is headed down the wrong path and I see how other countries do things better. I care deeply about America. It is the home of my birth, as well as my chosen home. It is also the home of my four-year-old twins and I am concerned that when they are my age, our country will have lost what is great. We blindly continue to "gift" ourselves with entitlements and rights we cannot pay for, entitlements that are beyond our means. Or, we take funding from Peter to pay Paul, which isn't quite how our Founding Fathers envisioned our progress.

That method is not fair, and strips us of our ability to find sound solutions to the problems and changes that need to be made. Today we are burying our head in the sand while kicking the ball down the road to future generations, rather than making courageous decisions to face reality. America today is headed toward a huge brick wall. We are gaining speed on that wall and when the collision happens, it won't be pretty.

The good news is that there is time to avoid the collision. We have election after election here in the United States where we can put everyone from a city council member to our nation's president into office. If we choose correctly, these are the people who will turn us around, who will put common sense reasoning back into our lives. We need to stand up and make our voices heard. That is needed now more than ever, and our Founding Fathers set up the structure for us to make these choices.

For many years now, we have had a number of well-intentioned people taking care of us. That is all well and good, but some of their strategies are odd, provincial, and poorly informed on a global basis. If I put twenty dollars in my own pocket, common sense tells me that I can't spend thirty. That is simple math. Why then, do we as a country continue to spend what we do not have? Why do we not examine monetary abuse in our system? Why is it that private enterprise is efficient, and government is not? And, why that does not alarm us?

If I put twenty dollars in my own pocket, common sense tells me that I can't spend thirty.

In another area, America in the 1950s and 1960s was one of the best-educated countries in the world. In 2014, however, Pearson's Global Education Index ranked the United States fourteenth out of forty countries in "cognitive skills and educational attainment." South Korea, Japan, Singapore, Hong Kong, Finland, the Netherlands, Ireland, and Poland are some of the countries that are far, far ahead of us. Why don't we take a look at what they are doing? Maybe we can use some of their ideas to catch up.

To make matters worse, according to Ipsos MORI (Market & Opinion Research International), the second largest market research firm in the UK and Ireland, the United States ranks *second* out of fourteen countries in general ignorance about social statistics such as teen pregnancy, unemployment rates, and voting patterns. Only Italy is ahead of us here.

So let's jump in and take a look at what other countries are doing, and let's consider doing some things differently than how we do them today. We will start by examining the easiest, most doable, affordable, and simplest solutions that will get us back on track. In addition to the solutions discussed in each chapter, beginning in Chapter 3, many of the solutions will also be bullet pointed at the end of the chapter. Consider these ideas a starting point. Later, we can refine the solutions to correct mistakes we inevitably will make in the future, but let's get started with the low hanging fruit. Let's get started now. We've got a lot to do.

Mark Werts
February 2016

1

The New Global World: A Conversation in Beijing

IT IS OBVIOUS THAT TECHNOLOGY IS EVERYWHERE. In the past ten years, technology has hooked up the world in amazing ways, and global news is delivered to our phones as it happens. We can even check the weather report in Helsinki or Shanghai with a few presses of our fingertip. And, all of this technology is relatively affordable. In just a few years, technology has us living on a different planet than the earth was before the Internet. The Internet has expanded our ways of thinking and given us the freedom to make decisions in a global context.

Here's an interesting tidbit. According to Pew's Internet Research Project, a nonprofit, nonpartisan research organization based in Washington, DC, as of January 2014, the most recent date statistics were available before we went to press, 90 percent of American adults have a cell phone, and 58 percent have a smartphone. Then, on August 9, 2015, *Fortune* magazine reported that the Apple iPhone has 44.1 percent of the smartphone market share, and Samsung came in second with 28.1 percent. Samsung has been steadily making inroads on the iPhone for the past several years, and that is an important fact, *because Samsung is an Asian product.*

You as an American consumer are already thinking globally, even if you don't realize it. Want a specific set of French dishware? It might be cheaper to order them from France? Shipping might also be free? Many of us place that order. Most however, don't understand the full impact that dishware order has on the world. As customers begin to think globally, so must American businesses. We must, for example, become able to make dishware as stylish and as affordably as they do in France. America, though, is not as friendly to businesses as other countries are. It often is harder here in the United States for a business to do business, than it is for a Canadian company to operate in Canada.

Many other countries also make it easier for businesses than America does, and many successful countries in our new global environment are openly friendly to business and new employment. They even encourage new business and entrepreneurship. It is hard to believe that we are talking about the difficulty of doing business in America now, since being business-friendly was a self-evident truth and a presumption in America's successful past. And, it was what led America to greatness. It was part and parcel of the American Dream.

Some time ago, I read an interesting passage in Porter Stansberry's great book, *America 2020: A Survival Blueprint* (Stansberry Research, 2nd edition, 2015). In it was a business offer to the reader. I'm paraphrasing, but the text went something to the effect of:

> *Here's the deal. You're going to start a business, or expand the one you have. It doesn't matter what the business is. I'll partner with you, as long as the business is legal.*

> *I will also demand that you follow all sorts of rules about what products and services you can offer. If you are one of the 50 percent that survive the first five years (numerous studies show 50 percent of new businesses fail in the first five years), I will continue to bombard you with all sorts of regulations, laws, obstacles, and impediments that will make doing business as difficult as possible.*

Stansberry's text went on similar to the following:

> *I can't give you any capital. You have to come up with that. I also won't give you any labor. That's up to you, too. But I will demand that you*

follow my many rules about how much (and how often) you pay your employees, and where and when you're allowed to operate. That's my role, to tell you what to do.

In return, I will take about half of what you make each year. Half seems fair, doesn't it? I think so. You're also going to pay me about 12 percent of what you pay your employees, because you've got to cover my expenses for developing all the rules about who you can employ, and when, where, and how. You're my partner. It's only "fair."

After you've put your hard earned savings at risk to start your business, and after you've worked hard for a few decades (paying me my 50 percent each year), you might decide to cash out, to finally live the good life.

As your partner, I want you to sell whenever you'd like, because our "agreement" says that if you sell, you have to pay me an additional 20 percent of the value of your business at the time of the sale.

I know. You put up the capital. You took all the risk. You put in all the labor. But I've done my part, too. I've collected 50 percent of the profits. And, I've always come up with more rules. That's why I deserve a final 20 percent of your business.

One more thing. After you've sold your business and paid all my fees, I recommend buying a lot of life insurance. That's because one of my rules is that when you die, unless you leave your estate to your spouse or a nonprofit organization (and if your estate is valued at something more than five million dollars), as of this writing you must pay me up to 40 percent over the five-million-dollar value. If you buy enough life insurance, it could finance that cost. Your children will appreciate that.

If you're one of the rare, lucky, and hard working people who can create a new company, employ lots of people, and satisfy the public, you'll end up paying me more than 75 percent of your income over your life. Thank you so much.

I'm sure you'll think my offer is reasonable and that you'll happily partner with me. But, it doesn't matter, because if you ever try to stiff me, or cheat me on any of my fees or rules, I'll haul you into court. That's how society is supposed to work, right? And me? I, of course, am the government of the United States of America.

I love those thoughts from Stansberry, because he is right. That's the offer America gives to its entrepreneurs. And our "leaders" in Washington wonder why we don't have new jobs. The good news is that I have solutions. But before I tell you what they are, I'd like to share a conversation I had recently when I was in Beijing.

Not too long ago I was invited to speak at the annual Beijing Fashion Forum, an organization that is supported financially by the Chinese government to promote the Chinese fashion industry. The forum was held at the Grand Hyatt Hotel Beijing and one of the main topics was multi-brand retailing (the selling of many different brands in one store). At this early stage of the Chinese shift toward consumerism for the middle class, this subject is of huge importance. One thing about the Chinese is that they are not shy about "borrowing" ideas and expertise from the west, and applying successful "foreign" ideas to their own economy.

This borrowing of successful ideas is something the west should do as well, and certainly is something open-minded Americans should do, as we are generally more flexible to novel ideas than Europeans. My Beijing presentation was well received and my four years of studying Mandarin paid off, as I greeted the four hundred members of the audience in their own language. I explained that I had learned Mandarin because my wife was from Hong Kong, her father from Shanghai, and her mother from Beijing, and I had been surrounded by Mandarin during the seven years we had been together. That's why I took it upon myself to try to master what would be my ninth language. Mandarin is slow going, as each word has four tones, and it takes a keen ear and an excellent memory to learn it.

I am not yet fluent and admitted so, so I excused myself after my short introduction, and asked the audience to put on their translation earphone devices, which allowed me to carry on in English. I was glad my audience seemed to like what I had to say, as I hoped I could help them move forward.

After my presentation I got together with my partners and our Beijing public relations expert, Nels Frye. Together, we came up with the idea of marketing several rising Chinese fashion designers in my Los Angeles based American Rag store. The Chinese love American products, so this was a way of validating the designers to the Chinese consumer. Then we would include the designers in our American Rag stores in China.

One designer is Zhang Chi, and while I was in Beijing, Nels arranged a media day to announce our American Rag USA/Zhang Chi collaboration, the launch of Zhang Chi's new jeans line, and his specially designed products for the American Rag store that is opening soon in Shanghai. We had five TV interviews the day after my presentation, and about twenty fashion magazine interviews.

The media day was a huge success, as Zhang has two reality TV programs in China, and owns one of the most fashionable Beijing nightclubs (complete with rows of Ferraris, Maseratis, Lamborghinis, Bentleys, and Rolls Royces that are lined up in front of his club). Thirty-one-year-old Zhang definitely knows how to seize the moment. He has a sparkle in his eye, and whimsically plays with an image of a gas mask in many of his apparel designs. This is an important symbol in China, as the pollution in Beijing is so horrendous that many citizens wear masks of some sort whenever they are outside.

Zhang Chi's father worked for the government, and during my trip, Zhang showed me the building where his father worked. After his own Chinese education, Zhang graduated from a prestigious London design school, and then went on to Italy to be a designer. One day a mindless Italian made a negative comment to Zhang about the "Made in China" slogan. "Who would ever want that?" the Italian asked.

The comment ignited a fire in Zhang, and he set out to become China's top designer. When it came to fashion, he was determined to make "Made in China" a symbol of prestige, rather than a negative detraction.

After our rounds of media, Zhang, Nels, and I jumped in Zhang's new Bentley and went to a restaurant to celebrate the victories of our day. We arrived at the Rosewood Hotel in Central Beijing, which had just been remodeled by a Hong Kong group. The restaurant was beautiful and understated, but as luxurious as anything I had seen in the west. Our table was in the middle of the restaurant, and there, Zhang's wife joined us, as did Peter Caplowe, my expatriate Chinese partner from the United Kingdom (UK). With great grace and courtesy our restaurant hosts placed two chairs at the head of the table, one for their esteemed American guest, and one for the Chinese host and TV personality.

In high school I studied Latin, and I remember the Latin saying *in vino est veritas*, in wine there is truth, so as the wine flowed, so did the conversation and the truth. We all recounted the events and successes of the day when someone came up with the great idea of bringing Zhang's reality TV program to the California opening of the American Rag Chinese designer store.

Zhang and his wife had never been to California, and had never "really" been to America. They had only been to Florida for a few days, but they shared with me their thoughts of the United States, along with what they had been told as children and what they had learned from American movies. It was all of great interest to me.

They told me about an America that was favorable to business, where anyone could make it if they worked hard. They repeated to me the so often heard "land of opportunity," and their perception of our low taxes. Their America was a place where all people lived very well. Zhang and his wife each carried a piece of America with them, the iPhone 6 Plus, and they held it in their hand at almost every moment of the day. This phone was a piece of their American dream, of an America that could do anything, of an America that helped promote their business activities in China, and that communicated globally. Indeed, I think the iPhone 6 Plus is one of the greatest ambassadors that America has ever sent abroad. Thank you, Ambassador Jobs.

I listened carefully to their impressions. Then Zhang, who is a communist, went on to say that China is exploding, and that "if you are confident," you can make it big. He was living proof. He did it his way and his way corresponded to today's Chinese society. He told me that the Chinese government wanted its citizens to succeed, that there were immense opportunities. People across his country were encouraged and honored by all—if they were successful. Taxes were low and regulations were many, but these obstacles could be surmounted, as Chinese throughout their long history have learned how to survive. Zhang made it clear that the entire Chinese society was on the move.

He then asked me about California and doing business there. I shared that for the past sixteen years there has not been one day where I was not being sued by someone under a labor board, or by some other litigious scam or con artist who felt entitled to something I owned. I told him how in California in 2015 we have more than four times the amount of lawyers as Japan does (roughly 35,000 in Japan as per the Japan Bar Association, versus 185,000 in California, according to the California State Bar Association, so there are a lot of lawsuits.

Then I shared that taxes for a successful person who lives in Los Angeles or New York City were 55 percent, which included 39 percent federal taxes, 13 percent state taxes, city taxes, social security taxes, Medicare taxes, Obamacare taxes, and FICA. Then, if the person is successful, there is an extra millionaire's tax thrown on top of the list. We can't forget property taxes and a 10 percent sales tax on retail purchases, either. After all that, unless this man or woman can afford an expensive lawyer to set up trusts, and depending on the value of the estate, the government can then take up to another 40 percent in death taxes.

I shared with Zhang that I had bought a building for my company seven months earlier but could not yet occupy it because there are so many rules and regulations (seismic, ADA, health and environment, occupancy permits, construction code updates imposed at each change of ownership, and the list goes on). I also told him that many US cities—including Stockton, San Bernardino, and Vallejo in California alone—are virtually bankrupt due to excessive pensions that were promised by politicians twenty years ago. Now the day of reckoning has come and the cities do not have the money to pay for them. Plus, one only has to drive on our roads to know that many of them need major work.

When it comes to education, GreatSchools, a nonprofit organization that develops profiles of more than two hundred thousand schools, reports that sixteen other industrialized countries scored above United States students in science, and twenty-three scored above us in math. In addition, our government creates inequality through well-meaning but poor policies of constantly creating debt and inflating our currency, which is devastating to the wage earners and savers of the middle class.

I told Zhang that I had even heard some of our officials blame our problems on the entrepreneurs and risk takers who employ the majority of the population, rather than on their own misguided policies that created our problems in the first place. I shared with him that in California, and in many other places in the US, most entrepreneurs I know feel that success and risk taking are no longer celebrated, that personal liberty is far less protected, and that free enterprise is not cherished as it was before.

Zhang Chi listened attentively. "Mark," he finally said, "that sounds like the old Chinese communism." We all laughed at Zhang's witty remark.

An essential part of humor is that there is an element of truth. The potential absence of freedom in the Chinese system scares me, but at the same time I was stung by Zhang Chi's bit of wine and dinner humor.

In addition to my conversation with Zhang, my wife, Amanda, and I were once invited on a VIP cruise on the Huangpu Tijan, the great river that runs through central Shanghai. We were in the front of the upstairs section of the tourist boat, in the section set apart for the elite, VIPs, and government officials, and were with the head of Chinese Maritime Customs. The man explained that the elite who graduate from the best Chinese universities work for the government, where in the west, and especially in America (according to Chinese perception), our best were in private industry, and only went into government work if they had to. He informed me that this was an essential difference between the two countries.

"The trouble with the American system is that you want to make the poor wealthy by making the wealthy poor."

On yet another occasion I was in a restaurant in Beijing with a higher up in the communist party who said, "The trouble with the American system is that you want to make the poor wealthy by making the wealthy poor. We in China, however, are different from you. We want to raise the standards of the entire society." The Chinese have found that Chinese capitalism works, and that there are many ways to accomplish goals.

But enough about China—for the moment. I have been blessed with work that I love. I travel globally all year and have done so for my entire adult life. In addition to China and Hong Kong, my worldview includes living in Holland, France, Switzerland, and Belgium, and, through my wife, I also hold a residency card in Hong Kong. I have business interests in Japan, and am developing a new business in Southeast Asia with stores already open in Bangkok and Djakarta. My partner is the Central Marketing Group, which is based in Bangkok. We have also given them our American Rag license for Thailand, Malaysia, Singapore, Indonesia, Myanmar, and Vietnam. We had two stores open in Istanbul, are in discussions with a large company in Dubai, and have had preliminary discussions with a government official in Kuwait.

Plus, I regularly buy products for my stores at trade fairs throughout Europe, Asia, Africa, and Australia. All in all, I have been fortunate to have been exposed to numerous cultures, economic systems, countries, cities, languages, and ways of conducting business my entire adult life.

Through my unique worldview, I have come to understand what is practical and works, and what makes good common sense. I have also seen what is impractical and doesn't work. In our new global world, why would America pursue an idea that has been proven again and again not to work in other places? Why do we so quickly forget our own lessons from the past? And why do we attempt solutions, such as penalizing taxes and burdensome regulations that have been proven again and again to kill growth and jobs. These "solutions" have already been a miserable failure both here at home and around the world.

We have also forgotten that it was the personal freedoms that were laid out by our Founding Fathers that brought about the wealthiest society mankind has ever known. Yes, we have gone off track, but most solutions to our problems are plain common sense. Common sense is something that is often looked down upon by the intellectual community, but we really should apply it to many of our dilemmas.

We also need to take a wide look around our global world, and apply some of the successful answers others have found to problems we face here at home. We can do this. There is no reason to lie back and be crushed by the inevitability of systems that don't work. America doesn't have to be in decline.

Let's take a quick look around the globe to see what works and what doesn't. We'll start with France. There, it is almost impossible to fire anyone. To some that might sound good, that it might insure job security and stability. But really, it cripples business. I have a French colleague in the apparel industry who lost his company because his license in Japan was cancelled, and as a result, he had to close a couple of stores in Paris.

The penalty to fire someone in France is the payment of three years of salary, so that's what he had to pay all the employees who worked at stores he had to close. Result: his entire business closed and everyone was out of work. When it is so difficult to fire an employee, guess what? You never hire anyone, and this creates high unemployment.

The result is that unemployment is rampant in France. Trading Economics, a company that gathers economic information on nearly two hundred countries, places it at 10.4 percent, but I believe that number is low. Many people have dropped out of the employment pool. Strife is rampant, and crime soars. Petty crime is everywhere. There are not enough police to monitor potential terrorists or those who commit other crimes. This I have personal knowledge of, as I have been robbed in France eight times, including a mugging attempt and having my car broken into.

Due to the regulation that makes it so difficult to fire employees, you can see that small start-up companies are at a huge disadvantage in France. That's why there are numerous sole proprietorships. (You can easily fire yourself.) But, family businesses still thrive, as do large government-subsidized enterprises. Family businesses work because you can lay off your sister. She won't sue you and bring you before the labor board. You can use your father during peak times, and then lay him off and let him help with the grandchildren. He won't sue you either. This is French common sense, and it thrives—in France.

Japan's system is no stranger to dysfunction either. They want full employment. It's part of their culture and homogenous society, a society with a strong sense of group and national identity, and little or no ethnic or racial diversity. They did the opposite of France, though. Japan prints money and subsidizes inefficient businesses so they don't have to lay off workers.

The only problem is that, according to *Eurostat*, a group that provides statistical information to institutions of the European Union, Japan's debt as of March 2015 is 243 percent of their gross domestic product (GDP) and their currency has dropped 40 percent in the last year and a half. That means everything they buy from outside their island is 40 percent more expensive, and their economy has been in a no-growth coma for twenty years. In Japan, there is a greater wealth gap between rich and poor than even here in America. That always occurs when you inflate currency and attempt to live on debt, rather than correct the inefficiencies.

France and Japan are not the only countries that have a monopoly on unwise policies, but there are a number of countries who do things better than we Americans. Canada, our neighbor to the north, does pretty well in healthcare. The World Health Organization reports that 10.9 percent of Canada's GDP goes to healthcare. Canadian healthcare, while not perfect, works far better than our disastrous "health care" system. Here in the US, Americans spend 17.1 percent of our GDP on healthcare, and yet our "system" is marginal at best and is the cause of constant quibble in the Congress.

How about some common sense? Why don't we adapt elements of Canada's health care system, improve our care, and lower our costs by trillions of dollars? Canada's system provides coverage to all its citizens. Under the system, people are provided both preventative care and medical treatments. And with few exceptions, all citizens qualify for health coverage regardless of medical history, personal income, or standard of living. There are no co-pays. As a result, Canada boasts one of the highest life expectancies (about eighty years) and lowest infant mortality rates of all the industrialized countries. Simplistic? Yes. Possible? Of course. It is already successful in the upper half of our North American continent.

Many countries are also much friendlier to business than America—and quite proud of it. Singapore does everything to attract business and allow capitalism to succeed. When their recently deceased leader, Lee Kwan Yew, took over in 1959, their annual average income was five thousand dollars. Lee was openly favorable toward business and did everything he could to create a positive environment that helped businesses succeed.

And guess what happened? It worked! Singapore's wealth increased ten-fold.

Another difference between America and other countries, particularly many Asian countries, is the issue of entitlement. An entitlement is a right. Here in America we have the right to free speech, to housing, to vote, to be educated, to health and medical services, to pick and choose fulfilling employment, to be paid when laid off or fired, and to time off. Many Europeans also have the right to work for ten months and get paid for thirteen, to the right of free passage world wide, and the right to paid retirement. The list goes on. But in many countries, especially those in Asia, you only have the right to work. That's it. Family takes over if there is a need for assistance. If you don't have family, well, sometimes you are out of luck.

When it comes to taxes, I think we can all agree that America's system is deeply flawed and impossible to understand. It fills volumes of unreadable books. Plus, the Tax Policy Center, a DC organization that provides analysis and facts about tax policy to policymakers, journalists, citizens, and researchers, reports that 45.3 percent of Americans will pay no income tax in 2015, which means roughly 55 percent of the people pay for the others. This promotes economic progress and self-sufficiency? This gives people a sense of self worth and dignity? Americans are an industrious people. I cannot believe that such a large percentage of our population is "needy" and needs to be taken care of.

Trillions of our American business dollars also stay overseas to avoid overly burdensome taxes. As an example, on July 22, 2015, *BloombergBusiness* reported that, "Apple Inc.'s cash topped $200 billion for the first time as the portion of money held abroad rose to almost 90 percent, putting more pressure on Chief Executive Officer Tim Cook to find a way to use the funds without incurring U.S. taxes."

The article went on to say, "Under current law, U.S. companies owe the full 35 percent corporate tax rate—the highest of any industrialized nation—on income they earn around the world. They receive tax credits for payments to foreign governments, and have to pay the U.S. the difference only when they bring the money home. That system encourages companies to shift profits to low-tax foreign countries and leave the money there. As a result, more than $2 trillion is being stockpiled overseas by U.S. companies."

In 2015, Ernst and Young, a global leader in assurance, tax, transaction and advisory services detailed what I know from personal experience: Hong Kong has a flat tax of 15 to 16.5 percent, everyone pays, and guess what? In many instances they have a surplus of funds. My wife is a Hong Kong citizen, and several years ago we were surprised to receive a check after the close of Hong Kong's fiscal year that was described as a distribution of the surplus for the last fiscal year, so I personally know this occurs.

Hong Kong's tax system is equally and totally fair, and develops a sense of belonging because all citizens participate in the well-being of Hong Kong. Everyone pays his or her portion, however big or small, for government services. I am absolutely convinced that money would flood into America from all over the world if we had Hong Kong's flat tax, and if everyone felt a part of and participated in the welfare of the state. Immigration advisors in many Asian countries tell clients *not* to consider investing in America, due to the severe tax code. Common sense? You bet.

I could go on and on with examples, but let's jump right in. Let's take a closer look at the concerns of the American public, issue by issue, and discover fixes that Americans can rapidly employ.

2

The Founding Fathers

WHENEVER YOU TRAVEL SOMEPLACE NEW, IT IS essential to have a map to show you where to go. That's the only way to judge if you are making progress in the right direction. If you happen to get lost or take a wrong turn, you can quickly get back on track if you refer to your original map.

So before we begin our journey through the issues in this book, let's pause to refer to America's original map to see how we are progressing toward the ever-unfolding vision of our Founding Fathers. These are the men who developed our original road map, and pointed us toward our destination.

The Founding Fathers. Who were they exactly? Well, they were men who lived in a very different era, under much different circumstances than we do today. They didn't have computers, jet airplanes, televisions, telephones, or even electricity. What they did have was vision, a profound sense of purpose, a moral compass, and a deep-rooted value system. They were a large and diverse group of landowners, farmers, scientists, and merchants—and many of them had studied law. Most held some sort of religious belief, and to some degree, most were educated.

If you look up "Founding Fathers USA" on the Internet, a number of websites have a biography of each person who signed the Declaration of Independence, the Bill of Rights, the Articles of Confederation, the Constitution and its amendments. (You can also find Founding Fathers information in Appendix C of this book.)

The mini-biographies on the various websites make for interesting reading and give the essence of what many of the Founding Fathers thought, and of their beliefs. Indeed, you will even find the road map they constructed for what we today know as the United States, because they formed a union of what previously were individual states. Many of the Founding Fathers had worked on forming the state, state charter, and government of the state he lived in. Working on the state level, even back then, was excellent preparation for national level challenges. It is important to recall that the states formed the federal government, not the other way around.

Like people in any group, some of the fathers you would have liked, some were nondescript, and others were extraordinary visionaries. You will hear a lot about the Founding Fathers in coming pages, so let's look at a few statements and quotes from them to compare their thoughts and vision with how our journey is progressing today.

> **It is important to recall that the states formed the federal government, not the other way around.**

The fourth president of the newly formed United States is one of my favorite Founding Fathers. James Madison was a true visionary, a powerful thinker, and a realistic "two feet on the ground" type of guy. Later in his life, his association with an unpopular war, the War of 1812, tarnished his reputation and he lost his popularity with the American people.

James Madison

Federal Constitutional Convention - 1787, Master Builder of the Constitution, Fourth President of the United States (1809-1817)

Enlightened statesmen will not always be at the helm.

Charity is no part of the legislative duty of the government.

I go to the principle that a public debt is a public curse.

If Tyranny and Oppression come to this land, it will be in the guise of fighting a foreign enemy.

In framing a government, which is to be administered by men over men, the great difficulty lies in this: you must first enable the government to control the governed, and in the next place, oblige it to control itself.

It is a universal truth that the loss of liberty at home is to be charged to the provisions against danger, real or pretended, from abroad.

It will be of little avail to the people that the laws are made by men of their own choice if the laws be so voluminous that they cannot be read, or so incoherent that they cannot be understood.

No nation could preserve its freedom in the midst of continual warfare.

Philosophy is common sense with big words.

Religion and Government will both exist in greater purity the less they are mixed together.

The advancement and diffusion of knowledge is the only guardian of true liberty.

The apportionment of taxes on the various descriptions of property is an act which seems to require the most exact impartiality; yet there is, perhaps, no legislative act in which greater opportunity and temptation are given to a predominant party to trample on the rules of justice.

Every shilling which they overburden the inferior number is a shilling saved to their own pockets.

The circulation of confidence is better than the circulation of money.

The Constitution preserves the advantage of being armed which Americans possess over the people of almost every other nation where the governments are afraid to trust the people with arms.

The rights of persons, and the rights of property, are the objects, for the protection of which government was instituted.

The truth is that all men having power ought to be mistrusted.

There is nothing stable but heaven and the Constitution.

Whenever a youth is ascertained to possess talents meriting an education which his parents cannot afford, he should be carried forward at the public expense.

Isn't it interesting that Madison foresaw many of the issues we now face in America today? Looking around our new global society, the free societies (societies that embrace increased personal freedoms) are the most successful countries economically. The countries that restrict freedom are typically in some state of economic decline. Madison foresaw this as shown, by his various quotes. He warned us to be vigilant.

Thomas Jefferson

Author, Declaration of Independence, Third President of the United States (1801-1809)

I hope our wisdom will grow with our power, and teach us, that the less we use our power the greater it will be.

I sincerely believe that banking establishments are more dangerous than standing armies, and that the principle of spending money to be paid by posterity, and the name of funding, is but swindling futurity on a large scale.

If there be one principle more deeply rooted than any other in the mind of every American, it is that we should have nothing to do with conquest.

We must not let our rulers load us with perpetual debt.

Peace, commerce and honest friendship with all nations; entangling alliances with none.

There is a natural aristocracy among men. The grounds of this are virtue and talents.

We hold these truths to be sacred and undeniable; that all men are created equal and independent, that from that equal creation they deserve rights inherent and inalienable, among which are the preservation of life, and liberty, and the pursuit of happiness.

It is incumbent on every generation to pay its own debt as it goes. A principle which if acted on would save one half of the wars of the world.

Thomas Jefferson also anticipated many of our present day issues, and his quotes from more than two hundred years ago could be directed to our present day American leaders and candidates for future office. Long ago he admonished us to use wisdom and force sparingly, and against foreign conquest. He advocated peace, commerce, no entangling alliances, fiscal soundness, and called sacred the preservation of life, liberty, and the individual's pursuit of happiness.

Our American leaders obviously have not kept Jefferson's admonitions at the forefront of their minds, as we are wallowing in debt and paying interest on that debt by incurring even more debt. All of this will be passed on to future generations—unless we do something about it now. Plus, we are in a perpetual state of foreign conquest, and personal liberties are being removed from American citizens at an alarming rate.

John Adams
Vice President, Diplomat, Continental Congress, Second President of the United States (1797-1801)

Government is instituted for the common good; for the protection, safety, prosperity, and happiness of the people; and not for profit, honor or private interest of any one man, family of class of men; therefore, the people alone have an incontestable, unalienable, and indefeasible right to institute government; and to reform, alter, or totally change the same, when their protection, safety, prosperity and happiness require it.

Children should be educated and instructed in the principles of freedom.

Power naturally grows. Why? Because human passions are insatiable.

Property is surely a right of mankind as real as liberty.

Remember, democracy never lasts long. It soon wastes, exhausts, and murders itself. There was never a democracy yet that did not commit suicide.

Rulers are no more than attorneys, agents, and trustees, for the people.

The government of the United States is not in any sense founded upon the Christian religion.

There are two educations. One should teach us how to make a living and the other how to live.

We hold that each man is the best judge of his own interest.

These quotes from John Adams go to the core of American issues today, especially when he says, "Rulers are no more than attorneys, agents, and trustees, for the people." Why, then do more of us not participate in choosing these "rulers?"

A May 2015 turnout for a Los Angeles, California municipal election was a mere 8.6 percent! But Los Angeles is not alone. National and state elections across the US have voter turnouts that pale, compared to many other countries. Apathy is rampant because Americans feel their vote does not make a difference.

This is a dangerous situation, especially as Adams pointed out that the people have the power "to reform, alter, or totally change" the government, not the other way around. Too many Americans in our day and age have given up on the process.

Adams also said we should teach freedom from an early age to our children, which would reverse this apathy. The US government today does not equate property rights to personal liberty, as it should, and this also gives a sense of apathy. As do many of the Founding Fathers, Adams advocates separation of church and state, and warns in the strongest terms of the dangers of entitlements.

Patrick Henry

Patriot, American Revolutionary War, Attorney, Planter, Politician

Give me liberty, or give me death.

Somewhere during his or her school years, every American child is introduced to this quote from Patrick Henry. There are important reasons why that is, and these reasons should be at the forefront of our thoughts today. Life is liberty. Liberty is life. Our personal liberty in the United States has made us the most successful nation on earth. But globally, the new economically rising nations are adapting more liberty for their people while we chip away at ours. We also impose increasingly restrictive regulations on our job givers and creators, and on our entrepreneurs.

John Quincy Adams

Senator, House of Representatives (Massachusetts), Eighth Secretary of State, Sixth President of the United States (1825-1829)

America does not go abroad in search of monsters to destroy.

If your actions inspire others to dream more, learn more, do more and become more, you are a leader.

Impartial and unequivocal neutrality was the imperious duty of the United States.

Individual liberty is individual power, and as the power of a community is a mass compounded of individual powers, the nation which enjoys the most freedom must necessarily be in proportion to its numbers the most powerful nation.

Our minds are like old horses, you must exercise them if you wish to keep them in working order.

Our constitution professedly rests upon the good sense and attachment of the people. This basis, weak as it may appear, has not yet been found to fail.

Posterity; You will never know how much it has cost my generation to pre-serve your freedom. I hope you will make good use of it.

The best guarantee against the abuse of power consists in the freedom, the purity, and the frequency of popular elections.

The whole of my life has been on continued experience of the difficulty of a man's adhering to the principle of living within his income; the first and most important principle of private economy. In this country beyond all others, and in my situation more than any other, the temptations to expense amount almost to compulsion. I have withstood them hithertoo, and hope for firmness of character to withstand them in the future.

The first family to have two presidents lived during our nation's early years. John Quincy Adams was the son of our second president, John Adams, and learned government from an early age through example at home. The family unit and learning from family is a key concept for our new America if we are going to correct some of the wrong turns we have made in recent times.

John Quincy Adams told Americans who lived then, and now, to not go abroad to destroy monsters. Any student of recent American conquests will understand his point, and apply it to our concept of trying to bring democracy to the Middle East. He also spoke of leadership and the re-sponsibility of each American to lead in some capacity, as well as the im-portance of neutrality on a global basis.

His analogy of keeping old horses working to stay strong and current also applies to today's long-lived baby boomers, and the importance of stay-ing active and productive. And, Adams reminds future generations that free-dom is costly, and that our constitution is based on faith in the American people. He advocates frequent elections, so as to curtail the abuse of power, and to live within one's means both personally and governmentally.

Benjamin Franklin

Scientist, Common Sense Philosopher, Federal Constitutional Convention, First Postmaster General, and the first US Ambassador to France

> *It is the working man who is the happy man. It is the idle man who is the miserable man.*
>
> *Industry, perseverance, and frugality make fortune yield.*
>
> *If you can't pay for a thing, don't buy it.*
>
> *I saw few die of hunger; of eating, a hundred thousand.*
>
> *He that goes borrowing goes a sorrowing.*
>
> *God helps those who help themselves.*
>
> *As Pride increases, Fortune declines.*
>
> *Any fool can criticize, condemn and complain and most fools do.*

Benjamin Franklin wrote good, short, common sense admonitions that produce success and well-being. The success of America was also built on practical common sense solutions, and there is no reason to abandon the simple values that produced our success as a nation. Ben Franklin, and his many writings, such as *Poor Richard's Almanack*, are absolutely worth reading and remembering.

Remember, the working man is happy, the idle man is miserable. Social Security is on a road to bankruptcy, so let's move the retirement age to correspond to our increased longevity. This will also give us time to get our house in order, for as Franklin says, industry, perseverance, and frugality will produce fortune. He also wanted us to beware of our political leaders, not to go into debt, (yet another Founding Father admonishes us about this), and said if you can't pay for something, don't buy it. Good lessons, all.

George Washington

General and Commander in Chief of the Continental Army, First President of the United States (1789-1797)

A people who are possessed of the spirit of commerce, who see and who pursue their advantage may achieve almost anything.

Every post is honorable in which a man can serve his country.

Government is not reason, it is not eloquence, it is force; like fire, a troublesome servant and a fearsome master. Never for a moment should it be left to irresponsible action.

I hold the maxim no less applicable to public than to private affairs, that honesty is the best policy.

Influence is not government.

Mankind, when left to themselves, are unfit for their own government.

Nothing is a greater stranger to my breast, or a sin that my soul more abhors, than that black and detestable one, ingratitude.

Observe good faith and justice towards all nations; cultivate peace and harmony with all.

The administration of justice is the firmest pillar of the government.

The aggregate happiness of society, which is best promoted by the practice of a virtuous policy, is, or ought to be, the end of all government.

The great rule of conduct for us in regard to foreign nations is, in extending our commercial relations, to have with them as little political connections as possible.

The Supreme Court must be recognized as the keystone of our political fabric.

There is nothing so likely to produce peace as to be well prepared to meet an enemy.

Liberty, when it begins to take root, is a plant of rapid growth.

To contract new debts is not the way to pay the old one.

George Washington is said to be the father of the United States, but how many of us have forgotten that he said that commercial people who seek profit can accomplish anything. He also told us to be constantly vigilant of government, to be grateful, that justice is a firm pillar, and that liberty is a plant of rapid growth. Once again, here is a Founding Father who stated that new debt is no way to pay off old debt, and commerce, not politics, is how we should deal with foreign nations.

James Otis, Jr.
Lawyer, Political Activist, Politician

Taxation without representation is tyranny.

James Otis may not have been the first to utter the preceding quote, but the matter of unfair taxation was the straw that broke the camel's back for the early colonialists. In our times, US corporations keep trillions of dollars overseas, rather than expose those dollars to our tax laws, which are among the highest corporate tax rates in all the nations of the world. No matter what political views you have, if there were to be a referendum that asked all Americans if they felt we should have the highest tax rates on the planet, I suspect the answer would be no.

Thomas Paine
Political Activist, Philosopher, Political Theorist, Author of "Common Sense" (pamphlet), Father of the American Revolution

If, from the more wretched parts of the old world we look at those which are in an advanced stage of improvement, we still find the greedy hand of government thrusting itself into every corner and crevice of industry, and grasping the spoil of the multitude. Invention is continually exercised to furnish new pretenses for revenue and taxation. It watches prosperity as it's prey and permits none to escape without tribute.

Thomas Paine looked around the world of his time with wise eyes. The Old World was Europe, and he saw the negativity of greedy governments that taxed every aspect of profitable business. That excessive taxation is a restriction of personal liberty, which was the very foundation of the new American nation. If you get the opportunity, read his "Common Sense" pamphlet. There is much for us to be interested in there.

John Jay
Sixth President of the Continental Congress, First Chief Justice of the United States

However extensive the constitutional power of a government to impose taxes may be, I think it should not be so exercised as to impede or discourage the lawful and useful industry and exertions of individuals.

John Jay is yet another Founding Father who commented on taxation, and who stated that taxation should not impede the industry of individuals. It is interesting to note how united all the Fathers were on this issue.

▲

Many of the issues our Founding Fathers spoke about make them sound like they live in America today. But, most of these quotes were first spoken more than two hundred years ago.

So how did they know? How did these men foresee what was going to happen today? In reading these quotes it is clear that they took care to warn us. They tried to teach us. They knew about human frailty, and set up mechanisms so that when we failed to heed their advice and follow their vision, we could still get back on track. The most amazing part of this is that many of our Founding Fathers, those who signed our Declaration of Independence, were relatively young men when they signed.

Most would agree that in the past two hundred years we have strayed far from the path that was outlined by the visionaries who wrote our Constitution, Bill of Rights and Federalist Papers. For decades we have ignored the advice about personal freedoms, and have imposed so many rules and regulations that we are economically strangled. In coming chapters, we will examine this point further, and learn of several countries that increased personal freedoms for their citizens and also created high growth rates. These success stories from other countries will become some of our solutions for America.

Somehow along the way we made "charity" an integral part of our government, and presently 55 percent of our population pays the way for the other 45 percent. Ben Franklin admonished us to work, and that work creates happiness. All of the Founding Fathers had stern admonitions about the danger of debt, and said never to pass debt onto the shoulders of future generations. We didn't listen.

Separation of church and state is another area where we have failed to heed their warnings. Inheritance laws cover another of the many areas where we did not listen. So are the areas of foreign intrigues, the bearing of arms, entitlements, and education and its top importance to a successful society. Many of our incomprehensible laws of today create supreme power in the hands of the government. This makes lawlessness rampant, and renders the government not the servant of the people, but rather the master of the people.

If they could see us today, don't you think our Founding Fathers would turn over in their graves? But, they also foresaw that our current state of affairs might happen, and they put the mechanisms of the constitution, Bill of Rights, and early laws in place to bring things back on track. Yes, there are solutions. We *can* change things. As Washington said, we can accomplish anything, and with the solutions we'll discuss in the rest of the book, we absolutely will.

3

Freedom and Democracy

Democracy is the worst form of government except all those
other forms that have been tried from time to time.
—Winston Churchill

THE FIRST ISSUE WE WILL DISCUSS IS that of freedom and democracy. In general, I have found that countries that have more freedoms are wealthier, their citizens are happier, and their society is more efficient. These countries are also more capable of dealing with modern day challenges found in our new global society.

In taking a global perspective and stepping back to see the forest rather than the trees, nations that are increasing personal freedoms are on an economic rise, and those countries that restrict personal freedoms are in a state of descent. The Legatum Institute, a London-based charitable public policy think-tank, whose mission is to help people lead more prosperous lives, has documented this. The Institute also publishes an annual

"Prosperity Index," which is an annual ranking of 142 countries (the vast majority of all the countries in the world).

The Index is unique in defining prosperity as a combination of wealth and well-being. Understand that prosperity is not just an economic term. According to the Institute, prosperity is made up of eight areas:

1. Economy
2. Entrepreneurship and opportunity
3. Governance
4. Education
5. Health
6. Safety and security
7. Social capital
8. Personal freedom

In 2014, Sian Hansen, executive director of the Legatum Institute, wrote, "We need to recognize that freedom of choice and democracy are the building blocks of prosperous societies." This is how prosperity has become an integral portion of freedom and democracy.

From my numerous travels to China in the last thirty years, I have found that China (other than in the areas of freedom of speech and criticism of the government) is slowly letting go of the many restrictions and state socialism that has stunted its growth for decades. The country is even allowing an almost 1880 American *laisse faire* type of economic freedom for individuals and businesses, including foreign businesses.

Freedom of choice and democracy are the building blocks of prosperous societies.

Also, a January 20, 2016 *Wall Street Journal* article written by Lingling Wei and other contributors reported that President Xi Jinping's top advisors are sifting through reforms once championed by former US President Ronald Reagan and UK Prime Minister Margaret Thatcher for their respective countries. This is a main reason why China is on such a sharp economic upward trend. I have also personally viewed the prosperous transformation of the Chinese cities of Shanghai, Shenzhen, and Chongqing (the ever sprawling western Chinese city of thirty-two million).

On the other hand, with the exception of Texas, which is reducing regulations on business (and is growing at a 5.4 percent rate), the United States is imposing more and more stifling regulations, laws, and restrictions that inhibit our individual freedoms. According to taxfoundation.org, a nonpartisan tax research group based in Washington, DC, at 39.1 percent, America has the highest statutory corporate income tax rate in the world. As a comparison, countries in Europe have the lowest average corporate tax rate at 18.6 percent. China, however, is not too far behind us at 36 percent, according to a finance official in Hong Kong who is a relative of my wife's.

Note that this 39.1 percent is a different tax rate from the *Bloomberg-Business* article quoted earlier. The statutory corporate tax rate is the rate imposed on the taxable income of corporations (corporate receipts less deductions for labor, materials, and depreciation of capital assets). But, the corporate tax rate we usually think of is the tax a corporation pays as a percentage of its profit. The statutory corporate tax rate ranges from 15 to 35 percent, depending on corporate income, with higher rates (up to 39 percent) in some income ranges. Most corporate income is taxed at the 35 percent rate. If this sounds confusing, it is, and is exactly why we need to simplify our tax rates and laws.

When it comes to economic policies, the US also continues to lean toward the failed system of state-only decisions, which was the previous system used in China. In matters of political policy and restriction of freedoms, Chinese officials are politically appointed, and make decisions for the people. However, in economic matters, China is slowly abandoning this elitist process of decision-making, and letting the free market be the decision maker. Sadly, the US is going in the other direction, and well-intentioned politicians are slowly adopting the failed system that China is abandoning.

All this adds up to making economic prosperity and business in America extremely difficult. And, this is why the US, and its freedoms and democracy, will be in a state of decline until the trend is reversed.

Back to the Prosperity Index. Let's see how America is doing in the various areas, including freedom and democracy. The most current Index figures at the time of this writing are from November 2015.

#1 Economy

The first component is economy. America was ranked 11th out of the 142 countries on the list. Ranked above America, among others, are Luxembourg, Norway, Germany, and Canada. The top two rankings belonged to Singapore and Switzerland.

I have a problem with 11th. Maybe you do, too. America is still the world's largest economy, because we consume a lot. But at one point in time we were also the economic engine of the free world. We are no longer that engine, because our businesses are stifled by rules, regulations, high taxes, a government that is not favorable to business (and specifically small business, which is the origin of the majority of jobs in America), unfavorable international tax policies, innumerable barriers to start-up businesses, lack of capital and tax incentives for start-ups, impossible labor laws, prohibitive legal costs, government debt, and court systems that are dysfunctional.

If we continue to be surpassed by other countries, where all of these issues are handled more favorably, it does not bode well for our future. In fact, the consequences to the daily life that we enjoy will be dire, especially if our US dollar is no longer the world's reserve currency.

I did business in the 1970s in London right after the collapse of the pound sterling as the world's reserve currency, and the stories about the months long trash pile up caused by striking unions are 100 percent true. I also remember gas powered camping-style lights lighting the display windows in Harrods in Knightsbridge.

Due to the UK's economic decline there was limited energy in London and the southern UK, so the cash strapped British government, which could no longer pay its bills, placed energy restrictions on British consumers. Many homes and businesses no longer had power 24/7 and, according to the BBC (the British Broadcasting Corporation) inflation reached almost 30 percent.

In all its "wisdom," to maintain government pensions, and meet the demands of the unions and their refusal to accept less money in a declining economy, the British government inflated their currency. This decreased its value. Soon, the pound was no longer in high demand internationally, nor was it used as the world's reserve currency.

America is now headed down the same road, and the overall reduction of the American way of life could end up the same as 1970s Britain. If we keep on our current direction, the American standard of living will be reduced to conform to our declining economy. It's a simple concept. If America does not grow and advance economically, adjustments will have to be made to our more limited economic environment, just as people had to do in the UK in the 1970s.

Eleventh. What are the ten countries ahead of us doing that America is not? Certainly one of the answers is that they have more economic equality. The Legatum Institute reports that some degree of economic inequality can be a catalyst for growth, but our own government is the main creator of our wealth inequality. Just as the UK did, for many years our well-intentioned US government inflated our currency by printing too much money.

Yes, flooding the market with extra currency creates wealth inequality, as middle class wage earners and savers tend to become poorer. On the other hand, hard asset holders of real estate and stocks, and members of the financial world that handle sales of enormous amounts of money created by our government, often become wealthier. The fact is, when the government issues tremendous amounts of debt, it enriches those who make a living selling the debt, or placing it in the marketplace.

Many of our politicians admit that our problem of wealth inequality is growing. But never fear, they will come to the rescue of the dwindling middle class, and cure economic inequality by raising taxes on the job givers and entrepreneurs, and redistribute the wealth according to their own objectives. The politicians then cast these job givers and entrepreneurs as the cause of wealth inequality, and as greedy profiteers, while it was their own actions (and the Federal Reserve Bank's manipulation of interest rates and debt) that caused the inequality in the first place.

#2 Entrepreneurship and Opportunity

The second element of the Prosperity Index is entrepreneurship and op-portunity. The USA ranked 11th in this index, too, and was behind such countries as Singapore, Canada, Germany, and Iceland, among others.

We absolutely should be number one in entrepreneurship. Our coun-try was founded on principles of personal freedom, democracy, and op-portunity. So, why are we not? Entrepreneurship used to be our best strength, and at one time made us the wealthiest and most powerful nation on the planet. Our national anthem says we are the land of the free, but with all the restrictions we have in business I often feel that is not the case.

When I was in school, I remember learning about immigrants who arrived in front of the Statue of Liberty with tears in their eyes. This was because they had arrived from the Old World where there was zero op-portunity for entrepreneurship. Now they had landed in the New World, where, if you worked your ass off, educated yourself, and were disciplined and moral, everyone had an opportunity to rise to the top.

People in the rest of the world truly believe the American Dream is fully intact.

That was the classic American Dream, and you know what? In my world travels, I have seen that the idea of that dream is still alive and kick-ing in the minds of millions of people in countries around world. People in the rest of the world truly believe the American Dream is fully intact. This is a big confirmation that America needs to wake up to what's going on in the world today. We Americans, and our government, must realize that we have strayed from our previously successful path.

#3 Governance

The third element of the Prosperity Index, or as I think of it, the key to our freedom and democracy, is governance. There are three areas of meas-urement in a country's performance of governance: 1) effective and ac-countable government, 2) fair elections, and 3) participation and the rule of law. It is undeniable that effective governance will increase income. In governance, America once again ranked 11th, behind Finland, Australia, Canada, and just ahead of Singapore.

Yes, we did rank ahead of 131 other nations, but when we think of "effective and accountable government" how does The Patient Protection and Affordable Care Act (Obamacare) in it glorious, unreadable, and incomprehensible 1,024 pages fit into this description of "effectiveness?" Few people, if any, have time to read the entire Act. Instead of 1,024 pages, we need bills and Acts that we all can understand. How else will we know what we are supporting or fighting against?

Here's another. How does the twenty-three hundred pages of the Dodd-Frank Wall Street Reform and Consumer Protection Act, which was passed in response to the financial crisis of 2008, fit under the heading of accountable government? This bill regulates a bank's ability to lend money, and lays out laborious terms and conditions to lending, with the hope of reducing bank failures.

Contrary to the cautions of Founding Father James Madison, this is another document that is incomprehensible to the majority of American citizens. Most of us are only aware of this Act's negative impact when we obtain financing and purchase a home, or are refinancing a home and find that we have to sign eighty-odd pages of legalese and regulations. Most of us will never read any of the dozens of documents that conform to the Dodd-Frank requirements. But, we'll get writer's cramp when we spend an hour or more signing them. What a waste of productive time.

Laws that no one can understand puts the power in the hands of the government, and not in the hands of the people. Due to many such laws, only the government can selectively apply and interpret the rule of law. This reality causes arbitrary law enforcement on the part of the government. That, in my mind, is not democratic.

These kinds of laws also run against the wishes of our Founding Fathers. They might dismiss our many thousand-plus page laws as the equivalent of having no laws, because no one can understand them. These kinds of laws, by the way, are numerous. The IRS tax code alone consists of four million words and is four times the volume of the King James Bible. It is an absurdity. Why don't we just burn our tax code and start over?

A flat tax rate of say, 16 percent would engage all Americans in re-building the American Dream. This flat tax, coupled with a consumption tax that would be higher on those who consume more, would be fair. Let's say someone could afford a Rolls Royce. He or she would then pay a hefty consumption tax for this luxury, whereas the dude who has a modest Prius would pay substantially less. And as I previously mentioned, some countries such as Hong Kong, when they use a flat tax for all citizens, produce budget surpluses!

When it comes to fair elections and participation, which is part of the Index's 2014 governance area, we ranked 12th. (The Index can rank slightly different areas from year to year, so for this measurement we are using 2014 figures.) According to The Center for Voting and Democracy, since 1972 voter turnout for our national elections has ranged between 39 percent and 63 percent. Countries such as Australia, Belgium and Chile, all countries with compulsory voting, have rates that hover around 90 percent. And overall, the thirty-four countries that are part of the OECD (the Organisation for Economic Co-operation and Development) have voter turnouts around 70 percent. (The OECD is headquartered in Paris, France, and promotes policies that will improve the economic and social well-being of people around the world.)

Our state elections have an even lower turnout, and some municipal and local elections don't even have a double-digit turn out of voters. Surprised? I'm not. People in America feel that their voice is not heard, so it doesn't make any difference whether they vote or not. However, I have to agree with former President Ronald Reagan who said something to the effect of, "if you don't vote, you have no right to squawk."

The last element in the Prosperity Index's determination of governance is the rule of law. I have been an employer in the state of California for many years, and I do not recall one day in the last twenty years when I, as an employer, have not been involved in a lawsuit that is directed against my company, or me. I suspect it is not too different elsewhere in the United States.

Other than labor, personal injury matters, and family matters, the rule of law is only for the rich. Who can afford to go to court? Unfortunately, today Thomas Jefferson's vision of equality for all under the law is just that: a vision.

The City of Los Angeles currently teeters on financial disaster with crumbling infrastructure, potholed roads, financial insolvency (which has handcuffed the court system), and a reduction of public services. Yet, a large amount of the city's tax revenues go toward pensions and high salaries for city employees. Private industry could never pay these pensions or salaries without going bankrupt.

Today, Thomas Jefferson's vision of equality for all under the law is just that: a vision.

To compensate, Los Angeles has cut its judicial system to a shoe-string. One of the biggest cuts to the budget has eliminated over five hundred legal jobs, some of which were court reporter jobs. As a result, court reporters are not provided for most civil cases. The cuts also called for the closure of seven regional courthouses. Justice has also been delayed as a result of the cuts. Traffic courts, which were busy to begin with, now see long wait lines, with vouchers given to those who wait all day but fail to navigate their way into court. Fair and democratic? Not in my book. Scarier still are the two facts that this is some of what happened in Britain in the 1970s, and that Los Angeles is not the only city in America that is in this situation.

#4 Education

Education is the fourth subject on the Prosperity Index and America in 2015 was ranked 9th. This can only be because the American university system is the best on the planet. Our university system skews the overall American ranking because most of our lower schools—elementary, middle, and high schools—are sadly lacking.

Education is the key to peace in the world and understanding between diverse cultures, and it has the ability to make violence and war obsolete.

This is unfortunate, because education is the absolute most important element in retaining democracy and personal freedoms, and is an insurance policy for our children's well-being. Education is the key to peace in the world and understanding between diverse cultures, and it has the ability to make violence and war obsolete. Putting a focus on education is one of our most important simple solutions to our present day dilemmas.

#5 Health

Health and health care is the fifth key component in the Prosperity Index. The 2014 Index reported, "The health of a country is an important determinant of its prosperity. There is a proven link between health and economic growth, unhealthy people find it harder to succeed in school and in the workplace."

In 2015, the Index ranked America first in health, but America's low infant mortality was an important factor in this ranking. The Index also reported that America spends $8,895 per person on health care, with the average American living 78.7 years. Hong Kong, in comparison, spends $2,144 per citizen and the average life span of a Hong Kong resident is four years longer than that of an American.

Vietnam's average cost of health care per citizen is a mere $233, yet the average Vietnamese lives 75.6 years, just a few years less than the average American, and for a fraction of what the United States spends on health. Clearly, there is something wrong with America's system of healthcare and how it "invests" in the health of its citizens. From a businessman's point of view, America spends 97 percent more on health care than Vietnam does. Who can endorse this?

#6 Safety and Security

Let's move along to the sixth indicator, safety and security. Here, America ranked a low 33rd. Our Founding Fathers insistence that Americans retain the right to bear arms certainly has had an influence on the feeling of safety and security that is essential to prosperity, democracy, and personal freedom. In the new global world, few nations understand our Second Amendment, which reads, "A well regulated Militia, being necessary to the security of a free State, the right of the people to keep and bear Arms, shall not be infringed."

A militia is either a military force raised from the civil population to supplement a regular army in an emergency (such as the National Guard), or an organized citizen-based military force that engages in activities in opposition to a regular army. Our Founding Fathers wanted us to have the right to form a well regulated, or organized, militia to oppose our government if our government went off track. They didn't want one person to have the right to blow innocent people away with a dozen assault rifles. That said, I own firearms and am glad for them, as you will see in a later chapter.

> **Few nations understand our Second Amendment, which reads, "A well regulated Militia, being necessary to the security of a free State, the right of the people to keep and bear Arms, shall not be infringed."**

This misunderstanding about a militia is a reason for America's relatively low ranking in this area, because in most developed countries, citizens do not have the right to bear arms. America also has a huge land mass, and there are many woods, open lands, and farms and since our inception, rural Americans have owned guns. This is not the geographical case in Europe, and Europeans simply cannot grasp how it is possible that there are so many guns in America.

#7 Social Capital

The seventh area in the Index is social capital, which includes family, charitable intent, and trust. Here we were 11th, bested by countries such as Finland, Canada, and Australia. The Index reported that countries that have strong family bonds, charitable intent, and high levels of trust are also the wealthiest. If these three elements are combined, then the positive impact on our society is the greatest.

#8 Personal Freedom

The last of the eight factors is personal freedom. To me, the role of personal freedom is the single most important on the Index because it also ties into democracy. America's ranking of 15th was generous, to say the least, and is a testimony to the fact that the American Dream is still intact in the minds of people in other countries. If only it was so. Uruguay, Costa Rica, and New Zealand, are a few of the countries that ranked above America in this all-important area.

According to the Index, "Free people are more satisfied with their lives. Freedom also encourages economic growth, and economic freedom can stimulate calls for other freedoms."

This confirms what I have experienced in my travels, that economic freedom has the strongest relationship with national prosperity.

> **Free people are more satisfied with their lives. Freedom also encourages economic growth, and economic freedom can stimulate calls for other freedoms.**

If I were to find a single reason for the reverse of America's rise—and the cause of America's decline—I would look to burdensome restrictions and regulations that hamper the freedoms of Americans. Taking away our personal right to choose for our self, and our rights to ownership, to build something from scratch and retain the fruits of our labors, is just plain wrong. Our rights to leave our heirs our farms and businesses and the profits of our personal toils, is important to us all. So is the right to choose the lifestyle we want to lead and where and how we will live.

By imposing so many restrictions, our government has also taken away our freedom to fail—and the possibility to grow and learn by failure. Failure is an essential element of success, and I love the Thomas Edison quote, "I have successfully discovered one thousand ways *not* to make a light bulb." Obviously, through his failure, he also eventually became successful in making them, too.

When it comes to failure and helping those who fail, yes. Some people sometimes need a helping hand. But, handing out a free dole to so many without requiring them to undergo job training or skills assessment kills self-esteem, self-respect, and incentive. There is a very old Chinese proverb that says, "The best place to find a helping hand is at the end of your own arm." We built our country with this proverb in mind. This was the vision of our Founding Fathers: citizens being free to build their own lives—and they did.

Just so you know, I am all for helping the truly needy, including the disabled, the elderly, orphaned children, our veterans, and others in need. But Ronald Reagan had it right when he said that particular portion of our population, the "truly needy," could be about 10 percent of our society. According to several sources, we are currently funding over 40 percent.

Back in the 1930s, Franklin Delano Roosevelt initiated the New Deal, a series of domestic programs during the Great Depression. Historians now refer to the programs as the "3 Rs: Relief, Recovery, and Reform." Relief for the unemployed and poor. Recovery of the economy to normal levels. And, reform of the financial system to prevent a repeat depression. Roosevelt's intent, however, was that these programs would be temporary. Roosevelt even called welfare a "narcotic." Long term, he feared the programs would kill the American spirit of self-respect and self-initiative. But, eighty years later some of those programs are still in place, and look what has happened.

▲

When reading this chapter as a standard to judge how America is doing in our new global society, out of 142 nations, America ranked 11th overall. Things could certainly be worse, but in many areas we are in a state of decline and if this decline is not stopped we will continue to be surpassed by many nations in the rest of the world. And we also have to ask: are we fulfilling our real potential? What can we do better? Are we looking at the nations that are surpassing us?

One simple solution is that we should invest in ourselves and in our people here at home, and stop trying to destroy the "foreign monsters" that John Quincy Adams spoke of. America was founded on the idea of commerce, and here in the US there are "no limits to what we can accomplish," according to George Washington. Father George was absolutely right. We can do this if, together, we willfully put ourselves back on track as a nation.

We should invest in ourselves and in our people here at home, and stop trying to destroy the "foreign monsters" that John Quincy Adams spoke of.

There are many other solutions to address our shortcomings. First, as many issues as possible should be addressed on the local and civic levels. This is where people have the most knowledge of the origins of the problems, and where the local city or municipality must allow local solutions and support them.

I also encourage you to attend your local school board, city council, planning, and park commission meetings. Vote. Get involved in your local community and let your local leaders know what you think and feel. Just as small businesses drive our economy, our local governments set the tone for what happens at the state level. Most people have never, ever attended a meeting of their own city council.

For many of the state and national solutions, I turn once again to former President Ronald Reagan. When he arrived in Sacramento as governor of California, he found the state virtually bankrupt. However, he recognized that private industry was more efficient than government and enlisted private entrepreneurs and community leaders across a wide spectrum of political beliefs to study the various issues he had to solve. These leaders were called "Reagan's Raiders," and one by one, based on their recommendations and his wisdom, Reagan addressed the origins of California's insolvency and slowly turned things around. He did the same thing when he went to Washington in 1980.

Another on my list of simple solutions is the flat tax coupled with a consumption tax that I mentioned before. A flat tax will set the tone of government by the people, instead of government presiding over the people. It will force us to scrap the incomprehensible IRS code, everyone will participate, and it will create a surplus of funds in place of the huge deficit we now have.

A flat tax is fair, and has been used elsewhere successfully. It makes everyone part of the solution, gives the entire population a wake up call, and a sense of pride and ownership. The wealthy will pay their fair share, but so will the poor and the middle class. Those who consume more will pay more consumption tax. Those who consume less will pay less. This will create a boom environment, and money will flow in. As a result, the world will focus on investing in America, and we will resume energetic and expansive growth. This flat tax can set a new standard for our new global economy.

I opened this chapter quoting one of my favorite thinkers and politicians, Winston Churchill. Here's another important thought from him for you to ponder when looking at the information from the Prosperity Index: "Criticism may not be agreeable, but it is necessary. It fulfills the same function as pain in the human body. It calls attention to an unhealthy state of things."

This flat tax can set a new standard for our new global economy.

We are fortunate to live in a democracy that gives us the freedom to analyze and criticize. Now we must take that criticism and turn it into something positive.

AMERICA'S SIMPLE SOLUTIONS

Encourage your lawmakers to let the free market be the decision maker, as this will jump-start our economy. Nations that are increasing personal freedoms are on the economic rise, and those countries that restrict freedoms are in a state of descent.

We need bills and Acts that we all can understand so let's encourage our legislators to be brief and concise, yet clear.

As per Ronald Reagan, if you don't vote you have no right to complain, so during every election, large or small, vote your opinion.

Economic freedom has the strongest relationship with national prosperity, so we must elect officials who will protect our freedoms and expand them.

We must get rid of legal restrictions that dictate how we choose to live our personal and private lives. Educating ourselves as voters and making our wishes known will make this happen.

The best place to find a helping hand is at the end of your own arm, so get out there and help yourself as much as you can.

As many issues as possible should be dealt with on the local level. Let's solve problems from the ground up and make our individual communities what we also envision for our state and nation.

Private industry is more effective than the government. We must encourage our leaders to look to the private sector for solutions.

We are a nation divided. To survive, we have to toss party lines aside and together find solutions. It is not you against them. We're all Americans.

Let's get people working on a flat tax right now. This will allow us to toss out the current incomprehensible tax code and bring the pride of ownership of our country to everyone.

Entrepreneurship used to be our best strength. We were the world leaders in this area, which made us the wealthiest and most powerful nation on the planet. We must proactively adapt changes that brings this back, as well as changes that support and reward our entrepreneurs.

Education is the absolute most important element in retaining democracy and personal freedoms. Parents must make education their child's top priority. If they do not, we will not be able to compete with other countries.

The American Dream is still intact in the minds of people in other countries. If we implement these simple solutions, the American Dream will once again be a reality.

4

Family

Destroy the family, destroy the country.
—Vladimir Lenin (father of the former Soviet Union)

AS THE FATHER OF FIVE CHILDREN, A HUSBAND, provider, and a devoted family man, one of the things I notice most when I travel from country to country is family. In every harmonious society throughout the world, family is of paramount importance. Indeed, there is even a Chinese proverb that dates from thousands of years ago that says, "If the family lives in harmony, all affairs will prosper."

I have found this wise proverb to be true whether it is a family of individuals, or whether it is a family of nations or various regions. Prosperity and a sense of well-being is linked to harmonious families, and while I try to avoid broad generalizations, the ascent of Asia today is, in large part, because this geographical area culturally holds family in a paramount role.

Certainly in China, both modern and ancient, the family is the center of the universe, and a source of belonging, well-being, personal security, responsibility, and love. Another nation where I had an office for ten years and came to know the customs and culture is Italy. Italy has survived and survived, and family is a central element to being Italian. I have numerous Italian friends who as adults living in the United States and other countries around the world call their families in Italy every single day.

Equally, the global Jewish nation has survived and flourished through the ages, and one of the central tenants of Judaism is the high value placed on family. Being in the apparel business most of my adult life in many countries, I can't begin to count the number of Friday night Shabbats that have I attended with the Jewish families of my business colleagues.

I believe that the primary caretaker of people should be their families, and not the government. Many governments are in the charity business and are supporting those who need help. This is best and most economically handled when done privately, or by a family. There always will be people who are truly needy or disabled, so one might argue that government is necessary to assume some role for them, but tight-knit, loving families should be the first to take care of their own.

Along with our new global world, one of the biggest changes is how we think of family. Family used to be mom and dad, two kids, with maybe some aunts, uncles, cousins, and grandparents thrown in. For the most part, all of the family members came from the same part of the world, if not from the same town. This is no longer true. People are making their own families out of foreign adoptions, close friends, marriages that span continents—and marriages and relationships that span races, ethnicity, nationality, and even gender.

Over the past four decades, the word "family" has been in the process of being redefined to include much wider circles of possibilities. This was documented in 2013, in a census.gov report, that showed that just sixty-six percent of households in 2012 were households of traditional families. This was down from 81 percent in 1970.

Also, between 1970 and 2012, the share of US households that included married couples with children under eighteen went from 40 percent down to 20 percent. During this same time, single person households increased from 17 to 27 percent. And, the average number of people per household declined from 3.1 to 2.6.

These are big changes over just a forty-year time span, and it is more than obvious that American families are radically changing. Indeed, this trend is an essential element of the new global society, and the new definition for the family. But, no matter how a family is configured, the central elements remain the same: love, self sacrifice for each other, education of the young, a mission of care for the young and the elderly, and a sense of unity.

My own family is global, and we resemble a small slice of the United Nations when we are all together. Amanda, my wife, was born of Chinese descent in Hong Kong, her father was from Shanghai, and speaks both fluent Shanghainese and Mandarin. Her mother is from Beijing and speaks only Mandarin. My experience has been that many people from countries with a large land mass don't tend to learn foreign languages.

Both of Amanda's parents survived the 1948 Chinese revolutionary upheaval and government transition to Maoism, but were only able to make their way to Hong Kong to start their lives over during the Cultural Revolution in 1972.

Amanda and I have twins, Iggy and Chloe, who are "hwin shway" or "mixed blood" in Mandarin, as they are half Chinese and half American. When we speak Chinese at home with Amanda's parents, little Iggy informs me that he doesn't "speak that type of English." Amanda was raised speaking Mandarin at home in the Cantonese speaking area of Hong Kong, but went to English speaking schools.

These many different languages did not faze me when I met Amanda and fell in love with her, but I realized I would have to learn my ninth language, as not everyone in her family spoke English. Now, a number of years later, I am still struggling with fluency in Mandarin, but am making steady progress.

Backing up a few years my first wife, Sidney, lives today in Pennsylvania, but I met her in Lausanne, Switzerland where she was a student. I was on my way to Madrid to enroll in the Universidad de Madrid when I was just nineteen or twenty. We lived in Spain, Switzerland, Belgium, Southern France, and the Netherlands during our fifteen-year marriage.

Sidney and I were blessed with two lovely angels, Julian and Zoey, my number one and number two children. Today, world traveler Julian lives in Cape St. Francis, South Africa, is multi-lingual, and recently dated a lovely young woman from Rio de Janeiro. Because of this relationship, Julian rapidly learned to speak Portuguese, his fourth language, and he's not bad in Spanish, which could be counted as his fifth.

Zoey is married to a man named Ike Pius, who is from Lagos, Nigeria. My two grand kid piglets are Ekena and Adora, who are truly as African American as their father is African and their mother is American. I recall an event last year where an older teenaged African American boy who worked with me had a chip on his shoulder. When I pointed out some of his sub-par work behavior, he accused me of being racist. I opened my iPhone and showed him pictures of my grand kids and told him he was right. I was a racist. That is, I am favorably prejudiced toward all races.

My second wife, Margot, and I married shortly after our son, Mark Olivier, was born in 1984. Mark Olivier was conceived in France and born in San Francisco. Margot was Dutch, from Amsterdam, and had occasionally worked for me during the eight years I lived in the Netherlands. She spoke reasonable English but we had many Dutch-speaking friends. Holland, being a small country, is made up of many polyglots so I came to find it normal to speak four or five languages, and many of our friends did as well. There was always a mosaic of languages spoken at home. When the telephone rang, I never knew what language I was about to speak.

Amanda and I married in 2009. I spent almost ten years being single, yet I stayed close to my entire extended family. We are truly a global family, with many mixed nationalities. Mark Olivier is married to a young woman from the Ukraine, the lovely Vlada, who is fluent in Russian. And, my grand kids, Ekena and Adora are older than their aunt and uncle, Iggy and Chloe, who are my youngest children. Yes, we live in a very new world.

Whatever the configuration, the main difference between family here in America and family in many other countries, is that Americans do not honor family and family members to the same degree as people in other countries do throughout the world. This is true when it comes to the Asian counties, especially those in the Far East. Asian cultures revere their elders and wisely consult their seniors on almost everything. And, advice from seniors is freely given, even when not solicited. As you can imagine, this can cause some stress in the family, but it also keeps important communication lines flowing. This is very true with my Asian family. Each person stays close and is involved in the life and affairs of their relatives.

Generations also mix more in other countries than here in America. Elders take care of children and grandchildren of working offspring, and many generations often live together in one home.

How many kids do we now have in day care across our country? The National Center for Education Statistics reports that in 2015 fully 57.4 percent of American four-year-olds were cared for in some sort of day care situation (12.6 percent being a government-backed Head Start program), while only 13 percent were cared for in their home by a relative. What might happen if some of our grandparents and great-grandparents took over the important role of childcare and we put the money we used to spend on day care toward educational activities for our children? I understand this will not work for every family. But in some of them it might. Let's always look at the successes of other countries; it is a good practice to begin to follow.

Family care of our children works well, as it also takes some pressure off our government in having to take care of so many people, especially our very young and very old. Our government is inefficient in this, so we need to develop a cultural shift that makes it more acceptable for our families to take care of their own. Unless western governments—and specifically the US government—get behind small business and really supports it, deregulates it, and gives it air to breath, our present economy might just make family care come about due to job losses. This, then, would be as a result of economic necessity, rather than due to an intelligent decision about determining what really works for our American families.

This cultural shift toward family also needs to extend into the workplace. According to a June 23, 2014 *Washington Post* article, the United States ranks last in every measure among thirty-eight countries when it comes to family policies. Not tenth or twenty-second. Dead last. Government-supported time off for new parents? Last. Employer-provided flexible work time? Last. And, according to a 2014 report by the United Nations' International Labor Organization, "Maternity and Paternity at Work," the United States is also the *only* industrialized nation that offers no paid maternity leave. Zero. We are also one of only three countries in the entire world that does not provide paid maternity leave. The other two countries are Papua New Guinea and Suriname.

If we are to compete successfully in a global economy, we have to improve in the area of family, and offer our families the same considerations that families in other countries receive. Only then, will we have happy, motivated, and productive employees. If our employees just mark time at their jobs, rather than enthusiastically provide innovative solutions, well, then we have already lost.

There are two other extremely important areas where family must re-assume the dominant role. These are national morality and pride of ownership. Let's look again to one of our Founding Fathers:

"The foundation of national morality must be laid in private families."
—John Adams, June 2, 1778, from his private diary.

National morality seems to be a rather broad subject open to personal interpretation, and with that I agree. However, I have experienced many religions and cultures in my global travels. As a result, I have found that the basis of most religions and cultures, and thus morality, is 1) that a spiritual world exists, and 2) that morality boils down to "do unto others as you would have them do unto to you." The Golden Rule.

This concept, The Golden Rule, should be taught in the family, by the family. You'd think it would be, but so many parents turn to the schools to teach their children morals and ethics. It is the family's place to teach future generations this one, single all-important idea, because when it is incorporated into a general population, there is harmony and peace. I have seen this happen in other countries, so why not here?

Secondly, our pride of ownership should be restored in America. Young and future generations should feel a great sense of hope, and know that with discipline, tenacity, and sweat they can and will accomplish their dreams. We have to create an environment to make this possible, and we can do this by restoring personal freedom, improving education, and rectifying our absurd tax system to a simple fair universal flat tax. Then when this has been accomplished, we can focus on restoring the rest of the vision that our Founding Fathers had.

Remember, it was their vision that what you earn and accomplish in your life should remain in your family, be passed on to your children, or to your new global family heirs. Here's a quote from the second president of the United States, John Adams, in a letter to Thomas Jefferson dated July 16, 1814: "As long as a property exists, it will be accumulated in individuals and families."

This was the intention of the Founding Fathers of the United States, and this is how it used to be in America. Unquestionably, this was an essential motivating element in our national success. Inheritance laws today, sadly and for the most part, have removed our motivation to succeed. They are blatantly unfair and must be changed. But before we make substantial change, because this is a large and important subject, we must give thoughtful consideration as to how we should proceed. Maybe we can get an updated version of Reagan's Raiders together to chart our new inheritance laws.

> **"The greatest inequality today is not inequality of wealth or income. It is the inequality between the child brought up in a loving, supportive family and one who has been denied that birthright."**
> **—Lady Margaret Thatcher**

Not convinced? Ask a farmer in the Midwest what will happen to his life's work, and that of his family, when he dies. Most likely, the farm will have to be sold. See if you find that resembles anything you might call fair. The fact is, our inheritance laws are just plain stupid. Entrepreneurs now have to pay large drains of unproductive capital for life insurance, so the business won't have to be sold in the event of an untimely death. The sale would have to happen because heirs generally cannot afford to pay all of the inheritance taxes that Uncle Sam wants. Is this fair? This is government controlling the people, not government serving the people. Our Founding Fathers would once again turn over in their graves.

I have one final thought about family from one of the greatest leaders of the twentieth century, Lady Margaret Thatcher, and it has to do with wealth inequality. She said: "The greatest inequality today is not inequality of wealth or income. It is the inequality between the child brought up in a loving, supportive family and one who has been denied that birthright."

The statement speaks eloquently for itself and for the importance of family and national well-being. Our families need to regroup. We need to hunker down, take personal responsibility for ourselves and for our own. We need to get government "for the people, by the people" reestablished, and demand that the personal freedoms that have been taken from us be returned. Only then can we reestablish the greatness that brought America to the forefront of all nations. Family has a key role in this process.

AMERICA'S SIMPLE SOLUTIONS

In every harmonious society throughout the world, family is of paramount importance, we must also have that priority here. This starts on an individual level, with you. Our elected officials should believe this, or we should not elect them.

What you earn and accomplish in your life should remain in your family, be passed on to your children, or to your new global family heirs. This will require a shift in inheritance taxes, which starts with calls to your legislators.

Young or old, sick or disabled, we must develop a cultural shift that makes it more acceptable for our families to take care of their own. This starts locally in churches, families, and businesses—and with your family.

The Golden Rule should be taught and practiced in every family. This, too, starts with you.

Pride of ownership should be restored in America. This can be done by restoring personal freedom, improving education, and rectifying our taxes.

5

Education

Education is the most powerful weapon
which you can use to change the world.
—Nelson Mandela, president, South Africa

A GOOD, SOLID EDUCATION FOR ALL OF our citizens is the ultimate answer to our many challenges here in the United States, and around the world. From national and international problems and conflicts, and the global hurdles that impede a fair and just society, education is the answer.

Imagine this: a globally harmonious, enlightened society, with an entrepreneurial bent that embraces change. This society would also create needed change, and enough personal freedom to enable all citizens to fulfill their individual potential. Sounds good, doesn't it? The best news is that this kind of society is within the realm of possibility.

Education takes time, consistent commitment, and patience. These are, perhaps, its biggest drawbacks. As a nation we need to realize this, take steps toward great education, and then watch the miracles take place. But make no mistake. Educating our children and adults is America's most important simple solution.

Educating our children and adults is America's most important simple solution.

In the United States we do education very poorly—and really well. Our universities are without question the best on the planet, and the rest of the world knows this. With reference to American universities, this is one of the areas where we have not totally lost the vision of our Founding Fathers.

It seems appropriate to again quote James Madison here. "Learned institutions ought to be favorite objects with every free people. They throw that light over the public mind which is the best security against crafty and dangerous encroachments on the public liberty."

To have their children educated in the United States at one of our many great universities is the dream of many parents throughout the world. These are not only children of global leaders in government and international industry, and children of the internationally wealthy and elite who will become leaders throughout the world, these are also children of everyday parents, just like yourself.

Just so you know, according to a May 31, 2012 CNN article, the number of Chinese undergraduate students in the US doubled from the 2006-07 academic year. The next year, that figure jumped again and by 2011, 56,976 Chinese undergraduates were enrolled in US colleges and universities. According to the Institute of International Education, a nonprofit organization that focuses on international student exchange, 274,439 Chinese students studied in the United States in 2014. That was the fifth consecutive year in which Chinese students were the largest national group among America's international student population. Today, China exports more of its students to the US than to any other country, even though their K-12 students far outscore ours in each of the STEM academics (science, technology, engineering, and math.)

I am on the Board of Counselors at the Roski School of Fine Arts at the University of Southern California (USC) and lecture on occasion at the Marshall School of Business, also at USC. Our former university president, Steven Sample, was a visionary who was aware of the desire of international parents to educate their offspring at US universities. With that in mind, he thrust USC into the realm as one of the top US research universities in the 1990s. How? By accepting a high percentage of highly qualified international applicants, which propelled USC into the ranks of one of the most difficult universities to be accepted into.

Indeed, until 2014, USC had the highest percentage of foreign students in the entire US, when New York University (NYU) took the top position. However, USC remains a close second with approximately 45 percent of its student body from countries other than the US.

In addition, the 2014 Open Doors Report on International Education Exchange found that the number of international students at colleges and universities in the United States increased by 8 percent, to a record high of 886,052 students in the 2013/2014 academic years.

Like so many things, the welcoming of so many international students to US universities has its positives and negatives. Certainly on the positive side, this phenomenon is reflective of our new global society. The best that can be found globally can now be had by just about anyone who can afford it. This works for any item one might want to purchase or consume. Buy a great pair of gloves from Amazon.com? They may have been made in England or France. Purchase an online subscription to a computer tutorial? That might have been produced in South Africa.

This new global way of thinking is certainly good for our university system, as it elevates the caliber of students. The pool of potential applicants now generates from around the world rather than just the US. This competition for university slots creates excellence, so the overall level of our universities continues to rise. If you have recently been admitted to a college or university, or just had a child accepted, you know that it is much harder today than it was thirty years ago.

Secondly, in an era of low or negative economic growth, bluntly said, foreign students pay more. They pay full tuition and these funds are needed by our under-funded universities here in the United States. This means fewer student loans, as foreign students do not qualify for them, and more paying customers. Our government is already burdened by too much student loan debt, much of which will never be repaid. This debt, of course, will be pushed off onto US taxpayers.

A third positive is that many of the world's future leaders will have an affection for and appreciation of America from their university days. They will also have first-hand knowledge of watching a democracy in action. Living in one of the world's most open societies, these students will definitely be influenced.

On the negative side, many Americans complain that our universities should be for Americans first, for our own children. They claim, and rightly so, that American universities are harder to get into, that they cost more because of the foreign competition, and that newly educated foreigners marry Americans, stay, and take many of the limited jobs available in the United States.

I have several simple solutions to these objections. First of all, we must all advocate for the expansion of education for everyone in the US, by elevating standards everywhere and at all levels, including the teachers and their salaries. Education must be a priority and to get the best teachers, we must offer the best salaries. Many of our top people go into sales, marketing, and other areas of business, we must entice them into giving back their knowledge and expertise to the younger generation, and money is an excellent motivator.

Yes, we should welcome foreign students, but our universities should also have a caveat that these students must spend three to five years after graduation in the United States making a contribution to our US society. Proven hardship conditions could waive this rule in the event of a family need back home, but the general standard will be to make a contribution in exchange for an excellent university education. We don't want people who are just "takers," we want givers, too.

And, having these great foreign students among us will educate our own students about cultures and customs other than our own in ways that teachers and the classroom cannot.

Personally, I find our visa policy of kicking out more than eight hundred thousand well-trained, bright potential entrepreneurs, scientists, engineers, doctors, professors, and people who are the *crème de la crème* of the international elite as soon as they graduate one of the stupidest policies our government has. It would be like the Los Angeles Lakers holding spring training for the best of the best for all the other NBA teams. The Lakers could teach them all their plays and skills so these other players could go back to their own teams and then pound the hell out of the Lakers during the regular season. The competition would know all the plays and strategy. This makes zero sense.

Oftentimes when I teach a class at USC or give a lecture, I ask the group at the end of the session how many are graduating, and how many would like to stay in the US. It's usually a mixed response, but there is definitely a large percentage of foreign students who want to stay to experience the "real world" marketplace in America.

This is a good thing, and could be an additional talent pool to enhance our areas of technology, science, entrepreneurship, and more, if only for a limited time. Sending the smart, educated potential immigrants home, and welcoming the international un-educated *en masse,* as we have done in recent years, is about as stupid an immigration policy as one can find.

As good as our American universities are, the American K-12 system is far to the other end of the spectrum. Our K-12 system needs a lot of help. There is an organization called the Program for International Student Assessment (PISA) that has measured the performance of fifteen-year-old students since 2000. In 2013, average global student scores in math ranged from 368 in Peru to 613 in Shanghai. The average US mathematics score of 481 was lower than the average for thirty-four developed countries, which was 494.

Plus, the National Center for Education Based Statistics reports that every year more than 1.2 million students drop out of high school in the United States. That's seven thousand kids a day. About 25 percent of high school freshmen fail to graduate from high school on time, and the United States, which previously had some of the highest graduation rates of any developed country, now ranks 22nd out of twenty-seven developed countries. If you think about it, it's scandalous.

In Los Angeles where I live, instead of teaching academic subjects, it might not be an exaggeration to say the first mission of public schools in the inner city is to teach the English language and to keep kids out of gangs and off the streets. I can assure you that such a goal is not even part of that kind of thinking in Shanghai, Hong Kong, Seoul, or Tokyo.

The same goes for the Scandinavian countries, Switzerland, Germany, and many other of our global economic competitors. Lack of education in America is the single most troubling area of our future. If we are to compete with other countries in technology, science, math, literacy, business, economics, and every other education standard we must educate our kids. This is an absolute must.

And while I see private enterprise out perform government bureaucracy in innumerable activities throughout the world today, one of the few areas where government has been, on occasion, equally efficient is education. As a society we must spend more on education, develop alternative teaching styles, value our teachers, pay a salary commiserate with a teacher's paramount importance to our well-being and advancement, and recruit the best teachers into the lower grades. We also need to make a family and social shift that values education. America's future depends on it.

As an example, 66 percent of US fourth graders across the country scored at a level that was below proficient on the 2013 National Assessment of Education Progress (NAEP) reading test. This means that they are not reading at grade level. Now, how can our kids compete in a global environment if they cannot read? And, how can they catch up when they are already so far behind. No wonder so many kids give up and drop out.

I understand this from personal experience as I was deeply distracted as a child, and didn't learn to read well until late in high school. Then I had to make a huge effort to catch up. That's why I get from a personal vantage point the importance of being educated, and having basic literary skills. Without them, you are at a severe disadvantage.

Even more alarming is that of students who come from low-income backgrounds. Eighty percent of low-income children score below grade level in reading. Reading proficiency among middle school students is not much better. On the 2013 National Assessment of Educational Progress (NAEP) reading test, roughly 66 percent of fourth graders scored "below proficient." Sixty-six percent. That means just one-third of our kids are doing okay in school. This is absolutely not acceptable.

In other countries, parents put far more emphasis on education. Parents save more for their children's college than parents here in the United States do. Parents overseas make the education of their children the number one priority for their family.

Here's something else one of our favorite Founding Fathers had to say on education:

> "Whenever a youth is ascertained to possess talents meriting an education which his parents cannot afford, he should be carried forward at the public expense."
> —James Madison, Fourth President of the United States

It's a matter of priorities. What's important to us? What do we value? And, what will make America prosperous, and arrest the present decline? It starts with a belief in people, and the value of their innate intelligence, and with family and society giving people the tools to develop their talents, and then the freedom to do so. Finally, we must be allowed to let people get to it, as Americans have done in the past.

I have faith in the talents, goodness, and international "street smarts" of Americans, and their abilities to find solutions, if we can only let them. A new emphasis on education will cost money, but we are wasting trillions of dollars "slaying international dragons," naively bringing "democracy to the world," and engaging ourselves in continual foreign adventures that costs trillions of dollars, as well as our children's future.

Let's turn America's look inward and bring those international dollars home. Instead of slaying foreign dragons that have not attacked us, let's put that money into educating our kids. Let's make America the shining beacon of light on the mountain that everyone wants to emulate. We can do it, but it begins, and ends, with education.

AMERICA'S SIMPLE SOLUTIONS

A good, solid education and a life-long love of learning for all of our citizens is the ultimate answer to our many challenges. To do this, we must recruit the best teachers and pay them top salaries.

Let's also welcome foreign students, but they must spend three to five years after graduation in the United States making a contribution to our society.

We also must look inward and bring international dollars home. Instead of slaying foreign dragons that have not attacked us, let's put that money into educating our kids. Had the trillions of dollars spent in Iraq been spent on educating our youth, America would be a very different place today.

6

Healthcare

America's health care system is neither healthy, caring, nor a system.
—Walter Cronkite

EVERY GOOD BOOK HAS ELEMENTS OF HUMOR, as laughter is an essential part of life. Healthcare in the United States is ridiculous and would bring full belly laughs if it weren't such a serious subject.

Not so long ago, I was required by a life insurance company that I had a policy with to have a stress test. This is a simple twenty-minute test that can be done in a general practitioner's office. First, sticky electrodes are attached to the patient's chest, shoulders, and hips. Then, wires leading from the electrodes are connected to the stress test machine. This machine monitors the patient's heart rate, among other things. When all the hooking up is done, the patient begins walking on a treadmill until his or her heart rate is up to 130 beats per minute. Then the doctor conducts various tests. This is clearly not as high tech as an MRI test.

As I had to get this done by a certain date I began to call around to various clinics in the Los Angeles area. To my surprise, I had very little luck finding anyone who would perform this test. It may have been difficult to find because doctors and hospitals might not make an easy profit by doing it. That is solely my opinion, however, as is the idea that our American medical system is based solely on profit.

Finally, in desperation as the cut off date was fast approaching, I called Cedars-Sinai Hospital and lo and behold, they did stress tests. Success! I scheduled the appointment and within a few days I showed up for my test. When I announced myself at the appropriate desk a receptionist gave me a clipboard with various forms to fill out, including all sorts of legal releases so I wouldn't sue them, even if I fell off the treadmill.

As I am over sixty-five, I have Medicare and a twelve-thousand-dollar a year supplemental policy with a hefty deductible to cover what Medicare doesn't pay. One might think that after paying a good portion of my income to Medicare during the many years that I have been working, that I would have total health coverage. I certainly had paid enough into the system. But no. Not here in the United States.

I turned in the clipboard at the desk and the receptionist made a copy of my Medicare card and a copy of my insurance card for the part that Medicare doesn't cover. Then I went back to my seat to await my stress test. As I was reading a worn out copy of *Time* magazine, an issue that was two months old, my name was called over the loud speaker and I was asked to present myself again to the desk.

The woman behind the desk informed me that they couldn't get my insurance company on the phone to get an authorization for the test. "No problem," I said, "I really need to get this done today so I'll just *pay cash* and turn in the receipt to my insurance carrier to be reimbursed." The woman looked astounded and repeated, "you'll *pay cash*?" It was as if I had suggested I was going to skip across the Grand Canyon. "Yes," I said. "I'll pay cash." At my words, she looked so befuddled that I almost felt sorry for her. She started to fumble around, and tried unsuccessfully to get someone on the phone. When she couldn't, she told me to take my seat, that she would get back to me as soon as she could.

I sat back down and resumed reading the worn out *Time* magazine. Within a few minutes, my name was once again called and I was asked to return to the same desk. This time the woman seemed a bit more in control and said that yes, I could indeed pay cash, but that the needed amount was thirty-eight hundred dollars.

Thirty-eight hundred dollars? Wow! I was more than taken back by the fee for the twenty-minute procedure and said, "I think there is some misunderstanding. I want to *walk* on the treadmill. I don't want to *purchase* the treadmill." After she insisted that the stated fee was correct, I told her I would take it up with my insurance company, and that I was going to leave. Then something very interesting happened.

The woman, whose name I never got, explained that she was Russian and could understand how taken aback I was, as she had been, too, when she first came to America. The health care system we have here in the United States, she told me, is very different from those in most other countries. "No one ever pays cash here," she said. "We are not set up for it."

After talking with her further, I understood that the "system" she spoke of was that my insurance company—as well as many others—only paid health care providers 20 percent of the full cost for many procedures. This hospital needed to make $760 from this particular procedure in order to offer it, and so they billed it out as thirty-eight hundred dollars, which no one ever paid.

I looked at this kind, Russian woman and said, "Of course. How was I so stupid as to not understand such a logical system?" Then I left. Eventually, after numerous phone calls to my insurance carrier, and repeated dialings of "1 800 wait forever," I got the approval to get the stress test, obviously less my deductible.

In another incident, my mother-in-law, who lives in Hong Kong and who suffered from terrible arthritis in her knees, flew to the US to have a knee replacement operation. This procedure is one of America's most common major surgeries. I happen to be a personal friend of Dr. David Golden who is a cracker-jack orthopedic surgeon, and the former doctor of the New England Patriots. He practices out of Cedars-Sinai in Los Angeles and agreed to perform the surgery on my mother-in-law. Yes!

The way my mother-in-law's Hong Kong insurance works is that it repays the insured for out-of-pocket expenses after a procedure is done overseas, after the final bill is submitted. So in we go, and my wife, mother-in-law, and I sit with the administrator of the hospital who tells us the price of everything, including a stay in a private room. It was going to be about forty-four thousand dollars. Other hospitals in Los Angeles perform this same surgery for as little as sixteen thousand, but my Chinese mother-in-law is in a financial position to want the best, and if anything went awry she wanted to be in a large, full-service hospital with every imaginable surgeon present and ready to step in.

She paid the hospital the full amount in advance, the surgery was scheduled, and I am happy to say that it was a total success. Not long thereafter, when opening our mail at home, my wife and I got a bill for $156,000! How was that possible? We had been told forty-four thousand dollars, so where was the misunderstanding? My wife and I talked about this with great concern and worry over dinner that night, as her parents had already returned to Asia. We decided that I would call Cedars the following day to see what it was all about.

The next day, the person on the other end of the phone nonchalantly said, "Oh, just ignore that. We had to send that bill to you to see if you would pay it, but you don't have to. That's just the procedure of the insurance company. Our bill has to be $156,000 in order to get the forty-four thousand that your mother in law already paid, and we're fine with that."

Puzzled, I asked if she was sure we could disregard the bill. She said, "Yes," and that was the last we heard about it. But what kind of a system is that?

I travel quite a bit and know from personal experience that doctors in many countries across the globe still make house calls to hotels. And, when I get the bill I always smile, as it is so much less than what the cost would be in America. That is, if you could ever get a doctor to make a house call.

Pills that cost two dollars each overseas cost forty in America. I recently had an interminable cough from my twin four year olds and was prescribed a cough syrup that set me back $130! How is it possible for a tiny bottle of cough syrup to cost that much? I lived in France for eleven years and never remember paying even a tenth of $130 for any kind of medicine, much less cough syrup.

Once, also in France, I was chatting with a French doctor and asked why French medicines seemed so superior to American medicines. This was from my experience in having medical care in both countries. He explained that French pharmaceutical companies do not have the long, stringent requirements and regulations of the FDA (Federal Drug Administration), and can get to the market faster. He also explained that in France there are not as many lawyers ready to attack if one patient in a million has an adverse reaction to the medication.

Maybe this was just one French doctor's opinion, but I know that if I had to get sick, I would rather get sick in France, Switzerland, or a number of other countries around the world, than in the US. My oldest son, Julian, flies yearly from his home in South Africa to Bangkok for his annual check up. He pays a fraction of the price for a full check up that he would pay in the United States and the hospitals are absolutely first class.

As we discovered in Chapter 3, healthcare in America is the most expensive in the world, and in my opinion, not even the best. We don't get what we pay for at all. Canada, Switzerland, Sweden, France, Italy, Austria, Thailand and even certain hospitals in India do health care much better, and certainly at more affordable rates than the US does. I don't care which side of the fence you sit on with reference to Obamacare, but one thing is certain, the 1,024 pages of this law are incomprehensible to 99 percent of Americans.

I refer back to the quote from James Madison in Chapter 2 where he says that laws made by men of their own choice are of little avail if the laws are so voluminous that they cannot be read, are incoherent, and cannot be understood. The Affordable Care Act certainly fits this bill. Some even argue that instead of 17 percent of our gross domestic product (GDP) to be spent on healthcare, under Obamacare it could go to 19 percent, or more than nine thousand dollars for each and every person in America. This seems nuts. There must be a better solution, and I think there is.

But before we get to some simple solutions to America's healthcare dilemma, let's review some of the countries that outperform the US. According to the Commonwealth Fund Health Care Report. They are Australia, Canada, France, Germany, the Netherlands, New Zealand, Norway, Sweden, Switzerland, and the United Kingdom. Among these nations, in the most recent survey, the US ranked last, as it did in 2010, 2007, 2006, and 2004. Maybe we should rethink what we are doing. Should our health care be privatized? Semi-privatized? Or, overseen by the government? Maybe we really don't have to reinvent the wheel.

Here is a simple solution that is logical and is something we can realistically do. Canada and the US share a common border that stretches thousands of miles. Toronto, Montreal, Vancouver, Calgary, and other Canadian cities are very near to many Americans. This means that on first sight, Canadians and Americans don't have a night and day difference, with the exception of the pronunciation of certain words. I am not saying that there is no difference, but as far as trucking and logistics go, America and Canada share the same continent. You can find such mundane items as Cheerios in both countries, along with thousands of other products that are absolutely identical.

I find that Canada has borrowed much from the US, but they also do a lot of things better than we do. Certainly the 11 percent of Canada's GDP spent on healthcare is better than America's 17 percent (and according to some, maybe even higher). America should adopt Canada's health system lock, stock and barrel, and if not, then do a hybrid of the already in place system on our shared continent.

So, you say, Canadian health care is socialized. That may be, but it works much better than our system, and more affordably. Plus, *everyone* has access to universal health care regardless of status, income, employment, health, or age. Even with Obamacare, that certainly is not true here in the US. And yes, there can be long wait times for non-emergency surgeries, but that means that people who really need care right now are getting it.

Another simple solution that is self-evident is, of course, health and medical education. Americans need to be aware that our current method of handling health care is nuts, that it needs to be fixed. We also need to educate Americans about nutrition as a means of preventative medicine. And doctors, believe it or not, need to be educated about nutrition, too. I have heard of several doctors who went all the way through medical school without even one class on nutrition. Out of curiosity, the next time you have an appointment, ask your doctor if he or she had any nutrition classes in medical school. The answer may surprise you.

In addition, we need to give strong tax incentives to grocery store chains to put stores that sell healthy foods into low income areas so people without a vehicle can walk to the grocery store, rather than buy their food at convenience stores that sell frozen and processed foods. We need to prevent and eradicate obesity by education, and by encouraging exercise in our kids. It doesn't stop there, though. Parents need to exercise, too, to set the example.

According to the Centers for Disease and Prevention (CDC), the rate of obesity among children and adolescents has doubled over the past decade and is now considered an epidemic. Their evidence also suggests that diet plays an important role in the onset of chronic disease. In particular, diets high in saturated fats, calories, cholesterol, and salt are associated with chronic conditions such as coronary heart disease, diabetes, stroke, osteoporosis, and obesity. Who wants that for their kids? Or for anyone they love, or even for themselves?

In this way we put the basics of health care into the hands of our citizens. Of course, it's been there all along. But if people do not know what to eat to keep them healthy, if, as children, they do not see good food choices being made by their parents, then they simply do not know what they should eat.

If we can educate our citizens to improve their diets, we can reduce instances of major disease, and also reduce health care costs. The best benefit is that Americans will live longer, healthier, more enjoyable lives.

Interestingly enough, a societal diet change is one of the easiest a country can make. Through intensive education (there's that word again), and by making it easy for students and low-income citizens to purchase healthy foods, we can see positive changes in just a few years. So let's do it. Let's do it now.

AMERICA'S SIMPLE SOLUTIONS

Let's adopt Canada's health system lock, stock and barrel, or do a hybrid of their already in place system. This could save us trillions of dollars.

Americans must be educated about nutrition as a means of preventative medicine, and this includes teaching our doctors about nutrition. Obesity and diabetes are out of control in America, and this is largely due to a lack of nutritional education.

America also needs to take a step back, appoint a private industry advisory board to study what other nations are doing more successfully than we are, and present proposals to our executive and legislative branches, concrete proposals that mirror the already proven successes elsewhere.

7

Religion

Religion and Government will both exist in greater purity,
the less they are mixed together.
—James Madison, Fourth President of the United States

The government of the United States is not in any sense
founded upon the Christian religion.
—John Adams, Second President of the United States, Signer of the
Declaration of Independence, US Diplomat to France and England

I WAS BORN INTO A STRICT ROMAN CATHOLIC family. My father attended daily mass his entire life, and this fact set the tone to my entire early up bringing. Priests and nuns were scattered throughout our extended family, and our calendar year when I was growing up, was basically the Catholic religious calendar. Lent, advent, the holy days of obligation, Christmas, Easter, and all the rest were taken to the dinner table for discussion every day. Religion was simply a part of life.

Going to church was an absolute must each and every Sunday, with novenas on Wednesdays. I made my first communion with the rest of the first graders, and my dad left annually to go on retreats with his Catholic brethren. Our home was also open to a variety of priests every Sunday night for dinner. Anything other than a total Catholic education was heresy, and a mortal sin. I knew nothing else until my mid teens.

In the 1940s Rev. Joseph Vaughan S.J. was a radio priest who spent numerous years in Rome as the liaison between the Jesuit order and the Papacy. This priest was also my uncle Joe, my mother's uncle, so he actually was my great uncle. Uncle Joe relished a good cigar, and taught me numerous card games when I was young, including poker. For many years he was the receiving party for Jesuits who visited Rome. During that time, he learned and spoke what I remember to be thirteen languages, including many languages of Eastern Europe, such as Hungarian and Polish. He also lived in Rome during the time of Mussolini.

One day when I was about ten years old I remember being in Blessed Sacrament Church, in Hollywood, California on a day when confession was held, and I remarked that a certain confessional had an unbelievably long list of languages hung on the outside. After taking a closer look I saw that it was the confessional of my uncle Joe. What a fantastic guy!!

My mother's brother, my uncle Dick, was also a Jesuit and was one of only several Jesuit provincials in the United States. "Provincials" is a term for the head of all the Jesuit priests for a particular area, or province. Currently, there are seven Jesuit provinces in the United States, although that number may have been different fifty years ago.

Uncle Dick was a clinical psychologist as well as a Catholic priest, and his PhD qualified him for high Jesuit administrative duties, which he always claimed not to like. I remember that when I lived in Amsterdam in the 1970s Uncle Dick paid a two- or three-day visit and we did a number of touristy things together. It was one of the rare times I got to spend a lot of quality time with him, as he had always been a bit distant with me. At that time of my life I wasn't a practicing Catholic, nor did I express a belief in structured religion. This was a problem for most of the religious members of my family.

Religion didn't stop with Uncle Joe and Uncle Dick in my mother's family. Her aunt, Sister Thomas, O.P., was a Dominican nun and president of Dominican College in San Rafael, California. My mother's younger sister, whom I called Auntie, was also a Dominican nun and worried about my soul well into her nineties, when she passed.

If there ever was a saint, Auntie was it. She took care of my elderly parents until they died, and this was no easy task as Mom had both Alzheimers and Parkinsons during her last fifteen years. But this is what religious people do. I have first cousins on my mother's side who are nuns and they do brilliant work even today. As you can see, I have seen religious faith in action my entire life.

If that wasn't enough religion for one young guy growing up, my father studied for ten years to become a priest, and then left the Jesuits to become a medical doctor (although he was educated in medicine at Jesuit Georgetown University in Washington, DC). His two brothers, Clyde and Hilary, were ordained Jesuit priests, too. Rev. Clyde Werts was head of the engineering department at Loyola University in Los Angeles and Rev. Hilary Werts founded a Jesuit mission in Hiroshima, Japan after the Second World War, and lived in Japan for many years. I remember Uncle Hilly telling me about eating raw fish when I was a tyke, and I think of him even today when I eat sashimi on my regular jaunts to Japan.

My older brother, Eric Werts, was an ordained Jesuit priest as well, but when I was living in France in the late 1970s, I got a phone call in the middle of the night from him. Eric must have been about thirty-seven at the time, and blurted out that something terrible had happened. Fearful that my folks had died unexpectedly, or that his news was something equally shocking, I insisted that since he had awakened me in the middle of the night that he couldn't hold back his "terrible news."

"Mark," he said, "I've fallen in love with a woman!"

Relieved that my parents were okay, I said, "That's wonderful news. Finally! It took you long enough."

But Eric replied that I didn't understand; he was a Jesuit priest.

"So?" I replied. I assured him that it was wonderful to fall in love and that he was very lucky to have done so. Eric later left the Jesuits and married Ruth, the love of his life, and lived for many more years. Each year he remained madly in love with her. Sadly, Eric passed away recently from Lou Gehrig's disease.

I, of course, went to Catholic grammar school, was an altar boy, attended Catholic high school, and my dad said he would buy me a car if I went to Catholic University. Ever the clever entrepreneur and *homme d'affaires*, a man of business even then, I enrolled in Loyola University, got the car, and then dropped out to attend USC.

As you might guess, I have always been the black sheep in my family. I mention all of this not to push my Catholicism onto you, but to let you know that I understand how important your religious and spiritual views are to you, because mine are important to me. From my upbringing I understand the all-encompassing vibe of religion, and that each religion believes, for the most part, that it has a monopoly on the truth.

Years ago my mother told me that if I was going to live in her home, I had to be a practicing Catholic. I said I understood, and shortly thereafter and without conflict, at age eighteen, I moved out and got my own apartment. Back then I was a licensed union truck driver and worked for Bekins Van Lines as a mover, so I made real adult money. I wasn't afraid of hard work, and could afford the results of my lack of structured religious faith.

I was then, and remain today, a spiritual person, but I understand why there are religious wars. I also understand the courage it takes to go against your family's beliefs. There is always a great deal of pressure and guilt thrust upon those who stray, and encouragement to "return to the fold." I can just imagine what it must be like to throw off the shackles of structured religion when your family practices a certain faith, and your city, state, and even your country's national laws are based on that faith.

Once again, education and worldly enlightenment are the keys that will bring religious harmony to a personal level, but that takes time. In the meantime, if you follow the Golden Rule, which is "do unto others as you shall have done unto you," what someone else believes religiously or spiritually should not be of great consequence to the overall world order.

As I travel, I see some sort of religion as an important part of every advanced and developing society. But what I also see, be it religions in

Japan, India, China, Thailand, Spain, Morocco, or Australia is that the Golden Rule is a basic foundation for each major religion, and as an extension, each successful society. The Golden Rule is a universal religious belief that is wound into the foundations of every formal religion that I have ever encountered, including Islam. Culture, history, geography, and climate all play a role in the history of structured religions, and we must learn to respect all faiths, as long as they play by the Golden Rule.

It's really quite simple. Government and politics should not be concerned with religion, because religion is a personal thing. Period. Just as beauty is in the eye of the beholder, religion is in the heart of the believer. And, you cannot impose your heart on another. There should be no "infidel," and no crusades to convert the heathen or non-believer. Mahatma Gandhi's life-long message of peace truly is the standard that we should all live by.

Just as beauty is in the eye of the beholder, religion is in the heart of the believer. And, you cannot impose your heart on another. There should be no "infidel," and no crusades to convert the heathen or non-believer.

As long as the Golden Rule is followed, respecting the spirituality and religious practices of your fellow man is what faith is really about. Our Founding Fathers initiated a separation of church and state for this very reason, and they respected the many early Americans of diverse beliefs who came to the New World to escape religious persecution. Today, the United States government should not be interested or concerned if their citizens do or don't eat meat on Friday, or if they pray five times a day, or if they do whatever consenting adults do in their bedrooms.

Freedom of religion means just that: freedom. As long as you live by the Golden Rule, and don't harm anyone else, government should have zero role in religious decisions. Keep church and state separate. Of all the subjects our many Founding Fathers spoke about, the importance of the separation of church and state in America was a subject where the vast majority of them concurred.

I owned a home in Amsterdam for almost fifteen years and found that the religious makeup of the Netherlands has held steady for a number of years. Roughly 60 percent of the people who live there say they follow some sort of religion. But, while nearly 30 percent of Dutch citizens are Catholic, only 5.6 percent of them attend church regularly, and there are many reasons why this is. It is not for us to judge, however. Holland has many old churches, and I remember a church on one of the canals in Amsterdam that had been turned into a camping store. The high ceiling of the old church was perfectly suited for the tall display tents.

The Netherlands might be overly social and a bit lax in its criminal justice system and church attendance, but no one can say that the country is in a state of moral decay. John Adams often spoke about the important role of "virtue" in a free society, and that a free society should live by it's constitution and the rule of law. The Netherlands certainly is a place where there are values, virtue, and moral respect for law and their fellow man. Who is going to chastise Holland for not having a structured religion? Citizens of this country impose their values on no one.

Some countries and societies, however, impose their values and use violence in the name of God and religion. Barbaric beheadings, crucifixions, lashes, removal of limbs, stoning, and other horrific "duties" are performed in the name of Allah, God, or some other sect or religion. People are killed simply because they disagree about things such as the identity of the true prophet of the seventh century.

The big question was whether it was a Shite or a Sunni who was the real prophet of God in the seventh century. This question is the basis of many and ongoing religious wars and the accompanying slavery (which is said to be God's wishes). In some of these people's minds, rape is supposed to be a holy act. This outrageous behavior is most often associated with religions and countries in the Middle East although it is not exclusive to that area. Genocides in my lifetime have occurred in Africa, Russia, Europe, Asia, and the Balkans, just to name a few. Many of these events were tied to religion, religious wars, or secular versus religious philosophies. Unfortunately, I don't think we'll be able to change this in our lifetime, nor do I think it is the responsibility of the US government to change the thinking of people in the Middle East or other areas. These tragic acts are a result of ignorant and ill informed people. Again, education.

There is another idea with regard to places where horrific acts are performed in the name of religion, and this one is a pretty simple solution. I was born in 1945. During the entirety of my lifetime, and certainly for hundreds of years before I was born, there has been a religious dispute in the Middle East. Since I was born, one American president after the other has tried to ease the religious strife of the Middle East, all to no avail. Today, religious differences in the Middle East are used as justification for our attempts to "slay foreign dragons." We Americans are also told that it is in our best interests to be there (because of oil), and that we must protect Israel.

To me, the Middle East is like a neighborhood. Imagine that you lived in a specific neighborhood and walked your dog at night. But, on certain streets, people threw rocks at you, planted booby traps that tripped you at night, and hurled insults when you walked by. This is a bad neighborhood and the solution is simple: choose another street to walk your dog.

Personally, I wouldn't go down that bad street unless I was forced to. If the bad neighborhood was to the right when I went out my door, I'd go left. Yes, not everyone in the bad neighborhood is throwing rocks or hurling insults, and you can stay friends with those folk, meet them elsewhere, email them, and plan secure visits, but you don't have to physically be in that bad neighborhood. Let the people in that neighborhood work out their own differences, but you should stay away.

When it comes to the bad neighborhoods of the Middle East, it is hard to separate the issues of religion and oil, as they are so closely tied together. But, do we really *have* to go to a bad neighborhood because of our interest in oil? Do we *have* to try to bring Democracy to an area that doesn't want it, and hasn't for the last five thousand years? Guess what, America became the largest oil producer in the world in May of 2014. Let's use our own oil and energy.

Fact is, there are numerous alternative energies, to quote a dear friend of mine, Paul Polizzotto, a division president at CBS who is also an avid environmentalist, "God gave us the winds, the oceans, and the greatest energy source of them all the Sun, and all we do is dig a hole and burn old fossil fuels. God is disappointed in our lack of creativity and ingenuity." I agree with Paul. Americans can do anything they put their minds to.

Protect Israel? Yes, for sure. Democracies support democracies. But Israel has to live by the universal religion of The Golden Rule, too: do unto others as you would have them do unto you. It is my view, and that of many other Americans, that Palestinians have the right to their own state. But if they get that state, and America financially supports their statehood and development, they can't throw rocks at their neighbors. They don't get both: statehood and throwing rocks. Doesn't work that way. Then America needs to place a huge billboard in the neighborhood that reads DON'T MESS WITH ISRAEL AND PALESTINE so everyone knows the rules of the game. That way if anyone dares to mess with our two friends, we and our other friends in the neighborhood can back it up with stern action.

But we don't need to be there, and we don't need to spend trillions of dollars doing the opposite of what our Founding Fathers counseled never to do: get involved slaying foreign dragons. There are a number of quotes from many of the people who signed our Declaration of Independence pleading with us, their future generations of Americans, to stay out of foreign intrigues, especially ones with a religious bent. We need to heed their advice. Religion and religious wars are not the affairs of our government. It's that simple.

John Adams, James Madison, many other Founding Fathers had strong views on church and government. And, contrary to popular belief, not all of these men were Christian. In fact, many, including Thomas Paine and Thomas Jefferson, were deists. Regardless of their individual faith, their wisdom in this area shines through more than two hundred years later.

> "As to religion, I hold it to be the indispensable duty of
> government to protect all conscientious protesters thereof, and
> I know of no other business government has to do therewith."
> —Thomas Paine, *Common Sense*, 1776

"[I]n politics as in religion, it is equally absurd to aim at making proselytes by fire and sword. Heresies in either can rarely be cured by persecution."
—Alexander Hamilton, Chief Staff Aide to General George Washington, First United States Secretary of the Treasury

"It does me no injury for my neighbor to say there are twenty gods, or no God. It neither picks my pocket nor breaks my leg."
—Thomas Jefferson, *Notes on the State of Virginia*, 1781–1785

So, what if we all respected and embraced the many different religions that are practiced here in the United States, religions that follow The Golden Rule? What could we learn about each other if we educated ourselves about how others worship? Imagine how much more closely our people could unite if we understood the differences that are already present in our country.

Most differences of opinion can be traced back to cultural practices and religion, so what if all the Catholics (gasp) went to a Lutheran church one Sunday? What if the Methodists spent a day with people of the Jewish faith? Or, if the Church of Christ people broke bread with the Baptists, and the Hindus got to know the Episcopalians? Maybe we could realize that we are not all that different. And, we could learn to accept the diversity that makes us great.

A solid, unified America. It is not that far away. All it will take is bringing our foreign interests back home and making solid, active steps toward learning to understand each other here. Come on America, it starts with each of you.

What if the Methodists spent a day with people of the Jewish faith? Or, if the Church of Christ people broke bread with the Baptists, and the Hindus got to know the Episcopalians?

AMERICA'S SIMPLE SOLUTIONS

As long as The Golden Rule is followed, what someone else believes religiously or spiritually is not of great consequence to the overall world order. We all need to remember that.

Government and politics should not be concerned with religion, because religion is a personal matter.

As per our Founding Fathers, if there is one principle that should be more deeply rooted than any other in the mind of every American, it is that we should have nothing to do with conquest.

There are areas of the world that are "bad neighborhoods." We should avoid entanglements, and engage in respectful commerce and friendship from a distance, and take care of our own needs, which we can do.

8

Immigration

The bosom of America is open to receive not only the Opulent and respected Stranger, but the oppressed and persecuted of all Nations and Religions; whom we shall welcome to a participation of all our rights and privileges . . .
—George Washington

IT'S NO SECRET THAT AMERICA IS A country of immigrants, and was founded on immigration. Immigration was the entire part and parcel of what old Europe called the New World. My family and most of the American readers of this book are immigrants or descendants of immigrants, or descendants from American Indians that settled here long before America was "discovered" in 1492.

Like just about everyone else in the United States, my ancestors came from somewhere other than here. I am of Irish descent, and also what is known as Pennsylvania Dutch, which is a mixture of German, Dutch, and possibly some folk from northern Flanders, the Flemish area of Belgium.

Almost everyone I know in Los Angeles, where I live much of the year, is originally from someplace else. Even states such as North and South Dakota were at one time filled with immigrants, populated by Scandinavians and northern Europeans who braved the cold, cold winters.

It is this mix of people from all over the world who basked in freedom, and created a great country through hard work and ingenuity. And in spite of our faults, America can still lay claim to being a great country. The many thousands of people who want to live here can attest to that.

And why not? Americans are generous and caring people, and we have elected well-intentioned leaders who naively give food stamps to 46.5 million people. This is, on average, 19.7 percent of our entire population. These same well-intentioned leaders have constructed and supported a welfare system that is easily abused, and thus, the good, solid tax-paying part of our population takes financial care of the all the others. They essentially end up paying all of the taxes for the many welfare recipients. Who wouldn't want to immigrate here?

We live in an age of immediate information, and the entire world knows how easy US welfare is to obtain. They also know how it can be abused. I have personally seen instances of this myself. Chinese immigration services often advise wealthy Chinese not to invest in America, but instead, to go to Canada, which is tax friendlier, and better assists new businesses with tax credits. Then they advise establishing a subsidiary of the new Canadian business in the United States, and to place their elderly family members in the US so they can take advantage of the welfare and medical systems.

Further, a front page article in the *Los Angeles Times* on March 4, 2015 by Victoria Kim and Frank Shyong, discusses the fact that birth tourism is an industry that is promoted publicly in China. Wealthy Chinese will pay up to fifty thousand dollars for help in getting to the United States for a short time. When their baby is born in America, he or she automatically becomes an American citizen. StarBabyCare.com, one of many such websites, claims to have assisted four thousand Chinese women have their babies in the US since 1999. Entitlement is the name of the game in America, and the entire world knows it.

No wonder we have an immigration issue. We made it happen ourselves. In the age of the jet airplane where almost anyone can travel quickly from a place that is in a dire economic situation to the United States, any person can work hard and transform from economic hardship to relative prosperity. Quite quickly, they can even be in a position to help their family back home.

It is no wonder that, according to the Pew Research Center, as of 2014 the US has somewhere in the area of eleven million illegal immigrants. The civil wars of Central America in the 1980s were such that it was far better to risk your life crossing the Rio Grande at night, than to stay in your home and be slaughtered. It is a complex situation, and there isn't a magic immigration fairy who can wave her magic wand and make justice reign. We're stuck with a situation of our own doing, so it is up to us to solve the problem.

Keeping families together is a core American value, and the idea to "send them all back" would be devastating to innumerable families who have children born in America, and whose children have American citizenship. Who will take care of these hundreds of thousands of children if their parents leave without them? The idea to "send them all back" is not economically feasible, nor is it cost effective. It would also devastate entire industries in the southern part of the United States, from California all the way to Florida.

A 2014 joint study from USC and the California Immigrant Policy Center found that illegal residents account for as high as 38 percent of agriculture workers, although the farming industry itself puts the figure at over 50 percent. Illegal immigrants also make up over 14 percent of the state's construction industry. You can also find illegals represented in large numbers in hospitality, landscaping, and any other job that requires physical labor.

Let's think this through. What would we do without these workers? Will you take their job? What about your college educated son or daughter? Are these largely minimum wage jobs something they are interested in? The fact is, illegal immigrants are a vital part of our workforce. So the "send them all home" scenario that is touted by some politicians to win votes and beef up their image is not all that valid. In addition to the question of who will replace these workers, is what do we do about the inevitable cost increase to our goods and services when they are gone? Few people want their jobs at the rate illegal immigrants are being paid. Are you as a US citizens willing to pay the inevitable higher prices?

Then there is the cost of moving everyone back across the border. Eleven million people, plus their legal children. We're looking at twenty million people total, maybe more. If it costs a very low estimate of three hundred dollars a pop to send an illegal immigrant home, that's a cost of six *billion* dollars. Where will that come from? And, how will countries such as Mexico, Guatemala, and Honduras absorb the heavy influx of people returning "home?" This whole approach of an enforced mass deportation is unrealistic.

On the other hand, I fully get what will happen, and the dire consequences to hard working Americans, if we leave our borders as insecure as they are today. Especially with the temptation of our ridiculous, incentivized, squashing welfare system. Our system desperately needs to be reformed to take good care of the truly needy, rather than those who are simply "playing the system."

When it comes to illegal immigrants here are a few facts that you should know. According to a November 20, 2014 CNNMoney article, illegal immigrants do not qualify for welfare, food stamps, Medicaid, or many other public benefits. Most programs require proof of legal status and, under the 1996 welfare law, legal immigrants cannot receive benefits until they've been in the US for five years or longer. In addition, according to a 2013 study by the Cato Institute, a DC organization that promotes public policy, illegal immigrants are about 25 percent less likely to receive Medicaid than their legal equivalents, and they are 37 percent less likely to receive food stamps.

Illegals also pay roughly fifteen billion dollars into Social Security every year, with little to no hope of ever collecting a single benefit. This is according to the Social Security Administration. Without these people paying into the system, Social Security would have been short in tax revenue as far back as 2009, and would have had trouble meeting payouts.

Collectively, according to the Institute on Taxation and Economic Policy (ITEP), a research organization that works on tax policy issues, our illegal immigrants pay close to $10.6 billion in state and local taxes each year. Contributions vary according to state, but in California the number is typically more than $2.2 billion.

On average, ITEP said illegals pay 6.4 percent of their income in state and local taxes. Also, a Congressional Budget Office (CBO) report quotes IRS figures that showed 50 to 75 percent of the 11 million or so illegal immigrants pay federal income taxes.

Then, according to the US State Department, there are about 4.4 million people who are waiting to get into the United States legally. Depending on the type of visa and the country of origin, the wait can actually be decades long. Many of our illegal immigrants wanted to come here legally, but either could not afford the fees, or conditions were so tenuous in their home country that they decided to risk coming here illegally.

All of this means that we need to rethink who we want and need in the United States. Do we only want the technologically savvy and educated? Remember that kicking out newly graduated foreign students from our universities is a travesty for our economy. The fact is, we need people of all shapes, sizes, colors, and skill sets who will follow The Golden Rule. These are the people we should welcome. Do unto others. Those who come from the "bad neighborhoods" should be encouraged to stay there.

Centuries ago when our country was new, people immigrated to America because they were hard working folk who wanted a better life for themselves and their families. This is still true today. But for our own self-interest, we must put our heads together to come up with a realistic, bi-partisan, amnesty immigration program that we all can live with.

Good, bad or indifferent, the Social Security system we have in place is based on the next generation being an active and productive participant in funding the retirement of the previous generation. It is no secret that Baby Boomers need lots of working young people to fund their retirement. If those new, young workers are not there in large numbers, Social Security will run out of money. Doesn't it make more sense to have Mr. and Mrs. Immigrant working legally here and paying taxes?

Americans are smart people. We can solve any problem, we just need the collective will to do so. So let's throw our political differences aside, face facts, and get our modern group of Reagan's Raiders together to develop a workable plan to make these simple solutions a reality. There are caring and humane solutions to our immigration dilemmas, we just need to make them happen.

AMERICA'S SIMPLE SOLUTIONS

Those who come from the "bad neighborhoods" should be encouraged to stay there. We can do this by securing our borders the way many other nations do. This is not an impossible task.

America is a land of immigrants, and for the foreseeable future will continue to be so. We need to accept this and set up guidelines to make immigration within America's favor.

The current ease of welfare abuse attracts the wrong type of immigrant— a "taker" rather than a "giver," a dependent mentality rather than an independent productive entrepreneur who is here to create productive growth for himself, his family, and the nation.

Our universities are the best in the new global world. We should expand our strength, educate our own Americans, and welcome foreign students here with the requirement of a three- to five-year period of "giving back," with a post graduation work visa.

The "send them all back" concept for illegal immigrants makes no economic sense whatsoever. We need to appoint a temporary, private sector committee of civic minded business leaders to study immigration issues and develop solutions favorable to private business and industry—with the motivation of job creation for the nation. We should also create a path to legality for those illegal immigrants who participate in this productive wealth creating endeavor.

We must also welcome the well educated, the talented, the entrepreneurs of the world who wish to create their own version of the "American Dream," and support them by the removal of strangling regulations and taxes.

Taxation

Black cat or white cat: if it can catch mice, it's a good cat.
—Ancient Chinese proverb used by Chinese leader Deng Xiaoping
in the 1980s to convince his government to decentralize and
deregulate the failed Chinese economy

MAKE NO MISTAKE ABOUT THIS: IF THE United States does not change its tax policies to a system of universal fairness, to a system that encourages growth and innovation, we will never arrest our decline. This decline was set in motion by the misguided economic policies of both our present government officials, and their predecessors. The good news is that our Founding Fathers foresaw our unfortunate situation of today, and more than two hundred years ago gave us the tools to make the necessary corrections. It's now up to us.

Here's what's going on. In 2015 we find ourselves with the highest corporate tax of any nation on earth. This is a most unfortunate fact, but it is one that is true. Once state and federal taxes are combined, Politifact, a fact-checking website that rates the accuracy of claims by elected officials and others who speak up in American politics, shows the average corporate income tax in the US is 39.1 percent. Then, there are additional state taxes in forty-seven of our states, additional city taxes (depending on the city), property taxes, city business taxes, sales taxes (which in California borders on 14 percent), and the list goes on.

In the event that you accumulate a fortune in this heavily taxed environment, the US government takes 40 percent of your estate when you and your spouse die. Let me clarify. In 2015, the estate tax exclusion was $5.43 million. So over and above that, 40 percent of your estate goes to the government. If you invest and are successful during your lifetime, you will also pay 20 to 25 percent capital gains tax.

In the 1960s a British rock group you may have heard of called the Beatles had a hit song called "Taxman," which ridiculed the absurd British tax system of that time. Since then, British tax laws have been reversed because they were found to be unfair—and they didn't work. Indeed, the higher the tax rate, the fewer taxes the government collected and the more man hours they had to put out to get them. These high British taxes hurt business, rather than assisting in growth. Clearly, our leaders in America never heard this song, and if they had, they did not have the intelligence to understand what the Beatles were saying. That, or they do not have an understanding of history and the many taxation systems that have already been dismal failures.

Included in our high-tax environment is a wealth inequality that was created and enhanced by our government's tax and monetary policies. This wealth inequity is often used as a justification for taxing the rich. We will examine the truth of this argument later, but for the moment, let's take a step back and look at the global environment that surrounds us, because this will shed new light on our unfortunate situation—a situation that needs to be reversed.

As a businessman who has tried to adapt many of the successful things I did in one country, only to discover that they didn't work the same way in another country, I learned that flexibility is an essential element of success. The Chinese premier in the 1980s, Deng Xiaoping, discovered that as well. And as Deng expressed, the color of the cat is of little importance, but the cat has to catch the mice. Not catching any mice? You'd better try something else.

In the 1970s, after the Chinese cultural revolution and the 1976 death of Mao Tse-tung (the chairman of the Chinese communist party), highly regulated centralized China lagged behind the entire world. Their economy was in shambles, and extreme poverty was the standard. It had become clear that centrally regulated communist and socialist economics didn't work. It all sounded good, but as British leader Winston Churchill so eloquently pointed out: "Socialism is like a dream. Sooner or later you wake up to reality." Premier Deng Xiaoping woke China up in the late 1970s and early 1980s.

I know this because I was doing business in Hong Kong in the 1970s. From Hong Kong Island, the mountains seen in the distance across the bay are part of Mainland China. In those days, any businessman who crossed the mountains into communist China had to be a real trooper. You brought your own food, sanitary conditions were abhorrent, hotels were funky to say the least, and if you went there, you got your business done and got out. It was not a pleasant world for the western businessman.

Back then I specifically chose to work with Hong Kong companies whose representatives traveled to Mainland China, so I didn't have to. I paid them a bit more, but that way I didn't have to bear the ordeal of traveling in China. What a night and day difference from today!

Thank goodness Deng Xiaoping instigated so many changes. He lifted the burden of over-regulation, and government planning off the shoulders of the Chinese people and gave them capitalism. Taxes were low, in some cases almost non-existent, and a "hongbao" could solve almost any tax issue. "Hongbao" is the Chinese term for a red envelope filled with cash, a common Chinese practice that rounds out any "sharp edges" and gets things done. In the west the "hongbao" is viewed as corruption, but it is a centuries old Chinese practice, and for Premier Deng Xiaoping, this was part of doing normal business. Business started to flourish, and as long as people didn't criticize the Chinese government, it worked.

The Chinese are an entrepreneurial people and their five-thousand-year-old language is full of references to making money, prosperity, economic well-being, plentiful harvests, and familial wealth—all glorifying everything communism is not. Indeed, when speaking Cantonese or Mandarin, to say Happy New Year, one says *Gong hei fat choy* in Cantonese or *Gong Xi Fa Cai* in Mandarin, which actually means "Congratulate you to be wealthy." Definitely, this is not a communistic saying.

This is why the Chinese, right away, took to Deng's move to capitalism, low or no taxes, and reduced regulations. Deng's judgment of Chinese culture and society was absolutely right. He plowed capitalism in fertile soil, and China, responding to the newfound economic freedom, quickly became a world economic powerhouse. Soon, they will become the world's number one economy.

They will, unless America learns from China's example. If we give economic freedom, low taxes, and fewer regulations back to our own industrious, entrepreneurial and smart American public, we might hold on to our number one economy. And if we do this, it should be able to happen quickly, because our Founding Fathers set America up with a government that serves the people, not the other way around, as was the case in China when China set off on its capitalist adventure.

I watched this transition in China first hand. My wife is Chinese as are all sixty-four members of her extended family, with whom I am in regular contact. I can assure you that capitalist China is still on a supercharged growth path, and will continue to be for years to come. The Chinese are disciplined, pragmatic business people who gravitate toward what is effective and what works. Free market capitalism works, and based on my personal dealings, and those of my business associates, the effective tax rate in China is 36 percent. This is compared to here in California where between state, federal, local, sales, and property taxes, a successful entrepreneur can pay in the range of 55 percent of total income.

Like Deng Xiaoping, I am not married to one specific way of achieving success. When in new territory, it almost always is trial and error, and every area of our fast changing world has now become a new territory. No matter what economic system you believe in, and believe me, there are many, as a businessman I too am only interested in what works, and what produces results, not a doctrine!

I have mentioned that in the 1970s I lived in Holland. This was when this socialist country had an effective tax rate of 93 percent. That is, there was 49 percent corporate tax, then to declare a dividend was 26 percent tax, and when the money passed to an individual personally, they could be taxed up to 73 percent. As the Dutch historically were against foreign exchange controls, money could be freely taken out of the country. So, two distinct economies developed in Holland at that time: the declared open official economy, and the black market, clandestine all-cash economy.

The funny thing about people is that they learn to survive. Highly penalizing tax systems, such as that of Holland, encourage people to cheat, because they must cheat to survive. During my many years in business I have experienced what works, and what is a disaster. Freedom and free market works, and government controlled socialism doesn't. It's as simple as that.

As an aside, parallel to what I experienced in Holland, has anyone noticed how many "cash only" farmer's markets, or markets of locally grown fruits and vegetables, have popped up recently in the US? There has also been an increase of "cash only" flea markets. And, I have noticed that in the San Gabriel Valley outside of Los Angeles there are ATM machines next to cash registers in the Chinese restaurants, along with signs that read CASH ONLY. Hmmm. I wonder why?

I saw all this before, in Holland. Incidentally, Holland's current corporate tax is 20-25 percent depending on the amount of investment and profit. The Dutch, too, are pragmatic business people and value what works. I am so glad that they have moved away from unfair taxation that actually *lowers* government revenues.

There are certain truths that are universal. For example, I remember studying about Pavlov's dog in a college psychology class. The theory is that if the dog barks and you give it a treat, it will bark again; whereas, if the dog barks and you give it a whack with a rolled up newspaper, more likely than not, the dog will stop barking. It's a bit simplistic, but this how it works in the real world. If a country allows people to make a profit, doesn't tax them to death, and lets people keep the fruits of their labors; if citizens are encouraged to take risks, and be innovative, allowed to be industrious, and rewarded if they are successful, and if parents can pass family businesses on to their children; if all of that is done, guess what? People will continue to do more. Deng proved this in China, and the system works anywhere, anytime.

To see just how well it works, let's look at the bullet train stations that are found throughout China today. As an aside, the US doesn't even have one bullet train. These newly built Chinese train stations are more modern, streamlined, and efficient than *any* airport in America. Before the Tom Bradley Terminal was renovated at the Los Angeles airport (LAX), anyone flying in from the futuristic Shanghai airport into LAX might have thought they had arrived in a developing country; the contrast between the two airports was so stark. This is because highly regulated, highly taxed economies do not prosper. But capitalistic economies, where economic freedom reigns, have the money and are able to invest in infrastructure.

Here's another universal truth: "Any system that penalizes success and accomplishment is wrong. Any system that discourages work, discourages productivity, discourages economic progress, is wrong. If on the other hand, you reduce tax rates and allow people to spend or save more of what they earn, they'll be more industrious; they'll have more incentive to work hard, and money they earn will add fuel to the great economic machine that energizes our national progress. The result: more prosperity for all-and more revenue for government."

This sounds like Deng Xiaoping speaking to the Chinese Politburo, but it's not. As one of my "once-in-five-hundred-year" men, I am quoting Ronald Reagan. Reagan not only brought down the Berlin Wall and ended the Cold War, reversed America's decline of the 1970s, ended the worst economic crisis post WWII in the early 1980s, and engineered a ninety-six-month economic expansion (the longest ever recorded in our history), he also restored confidence into the American people.

Reagan reduced taxes, reduced stifling regulations, restored economic freedoms, and let the free market take its course. And, within a few years of his election the US economic expansion was under way. Strange as it might seem, America must adopt, or better, readopt the policies that brought about China's resurgence into a world power and economic powerhouse. What is ironic is that Deng Xiaoping's new Chinese capitalistic policies were American to begin with.

Here's another quote that I find quite relevant. Not from a Founding Father, but from a wise man all the same.

> "We contend that for a nation to try to tax itself into prosperity is like a man standing in a bucket and trying to lift himself up by the handle."
> —Sir Winston Churchill

So here's where we are today. In California we have an effective 55 percent tax rate on successful business owners. There is also a 40 percent inheritance tax on assets a little over five million that you already paid 55 percent taxes on, so it comes to an effective rate of 65 percent, or more. Productivity growth is barely 1- to 2 percent, so there are few growing industries. Jobs, other than entry level, remain scarce.

I understand all the arguments about leveling out the business cycle and the importance of the goal of full employment. The monetary policy of the US tries to flatten the ups and downs of business cycles, because this policy displaces people and makes their jobs obsolete. People lose employment, businesses close, and lives are disrupted. I understand all the arguments for government intervention and regulations, but what really happens is the opposite of what was intended.

Recessions and economic corrections happen, but if we are nimble, educated, and ready, we can change with the times.

In a dynamic, changing world where technology makes everything obsolete in the blink of an eye, a business owner had better be able to change tracks quickly, or he or she will be out of business. And, workers and employees must be nimble and ready to evolve, learn, and change. It's just the way of the world today.

One of the best things about a free global market is that it is competitive, and the old saying, "if you snooze, you lose," is very true. A well-trained runner has to stay in shape or he will run in the back of the pack. It is the same with a business. Economies need adjustments, policies need to be shifted, and resources need to be placed where they are the most effective. Our American society must be educated, or educate itself, to anticipate the next step—whatever the next step is, and whenever it arrives.

Recessions and economic corrections happen, but if we are nimble, educated, and ready, we can change with the times. I have faith in the abilities and talents of Americans, but our government can't prevent change from happening. Change is also what happens when our government floods the marketplace with printed paper money that is not backed by corresponding productivity.

It's like this: if an entrepreneur has a wound in his or her arm, an infection, although it may be painful, the wound has to be cleaned to get the infection out. Put some disinfectant on the wound, bandage it, and continually change the bandage. All this in the short term can hurt. Or, the entrepreneur could leave the infection there, let it fester, and put numbing medicine on the wound. The pain is there and the infection remains, but it is not felt strongly. With time, maybe it will heal. Or, maybe not.

Change is also what happens when our government floods the marketplace with printed paper money that is not backed by corresponding productivity.

This is what governments do when they try to level out a business cycle. It is a painless process to print more debt. It is like administering an anesthetic, rather than letting the free hand of the market clean out the wound, start afresh, and reestablish growth that is based on the productivity of the new environment, and not on the issuance of more debt.

Here is where the issue of taxation comes in: The money for more debt has to come from somewhere and the easy-to-sell political answer is "tax the rich." This and many other entitlements have caused our US tax rates to skyrocket to the highest in the world. Just about anyone can get elected if they promise free money that will cost voters nothing. Unfortunately, this is a short-sighted policy, one that leads to zero growth, budget deficits, increases national debt, provides little foreign investment in the US, and generates low paying jobs and wealth inequality. In brief, it is exactly the situation we have today here in America.

Just about anyone can get elected if they promise free money that will cost voters nothing.

So where do we go from here? Is there a simple solution for this mess? Let me quote Sir Winston Churchill once again: "The United States is like a giant boiler. Once the fire is lighted under it, there is no limit to the power it can generate." So, America, let's light up the giant boiler. Let's correct this mess we're in.

As I pointed out previously, our IRS tax code is four times as long as the King James Bible. It is incomprehensible and we should burn it. Yes, that's correct. We should burn it. Destroy it completely and start over. Then let's initiate a flat tax of 16 percent, just like Hong Kong, who I might point out, has government surpluses from time to time, and constant and vigorous growth under tenuous political circumstances. Because of the folly of our eighteen-trillion-dollar deficit, we should initiate the US flat tax gradually over a nine-year period, starting in year one with a 28 percent tax rate for three years, dropping to a 24 percent tax rate for the next three years, then 20 percent for three years, and then eventually to the firm and fast 16 percent flat tax, all in.

We also need to legislate that our new flat tax cannot be changed or altered in any way for at least twelve years. Then, let's stand back and watch the huge miracles happen. Foreign investment will pour into the United States from all over the world, and especially from surplus rich China. China is holding trillions of dollars, and is actively looking to invest these dollars where it can't be diluted by the issuance of debt by the US government.

I predict with this new tax structure, that China will quickly jump to invest in the new America of restored personal freedom, low taxes, and a highly motivated educated work force that is on the move and wants to work.

Under this scenario, there won't even be 2 percent unemployment in the US, the middle class will have jobs that pay real money and offer future growth, entrepreneurs from across the globe will flock to invest in America, and the economic expansion will be such that Bill Gates's vision of no more world poverty by the year 2050 will become a reality before that date.

Let's stand back and watch the miracles happen. Foreign investment will pour into the United States from all over the world, and especially from surplus rich China.

A flat tax is fair. Everybody participates, both rich and poor. I come from a big family, a family of six children. My mother made everyone pitch in. To be part of the family, you had to do your part if you were to have all the advantages of the household. Same with America. Everyone will be part of the family of Americans and will claim ownership to our country, because they are participating in it. No more paying for so many people on welfare. In a family, if there is a disabled member, or an elderly person, the family takes care of them, but not the whole community, unless this truly needy person has no family, or the family resources are not there to support a severely ill or disabled person.

For the first nine years we could throw in a consumption tax as well. This is a fair tax, as those who consume more pay more, and those who consume less, pay less.

This is simple. It is understandable. It is fair. And, it takes into account the unfortunate situation that we have placed ourselves in today while gradually working ourselves out of it and toward fiscal soundness. Fiscal responsibility was an essential element of our Founding Fathers. This is absolutely doable, so let's get this ball rolling.

AMERICA'S SIMPLE SOLUTIONS

The United States must change its tax policies to a system of universal fairness, one that encourages growth and innovation, or we will never arrest our decline. To make this happen, your voice must be heard.

Remember that just about anyone can get elected if they promise free money that will cost voters nothing. Be sure to research candidates well before choosing to vote for them. Empty promises deliver nothing.

That flat tax we've been talking about? Once it becomes law, let's make sure it cannot be changed or altered in any way for at least twelve years.

Taxation should not be so high as to impede the industry of individuals. If a tax is too high, people find ways not to pay, or they become discouraged and we all lose productivity and jobs.

10

Voting

*The best argument against democracy is a five-minute
conversation with the average voter.*
—Sir Winston Churchill

WINSTON CHURCHILL WAS A FIERCE DEFENDER OF democracy and the democratic way of life, but obviously, from the quote above, he had some reservations about voting. He was an interesting fellow and I wish I'd had the opportunity to meet him.

Clearly, there are deficiencies in our voting process. Early on, our Founding Fathers had much discussion about who could vote. Should only educated men be allowed to vote? Or, should voting be opened to those who were illiterate? At what age could someone vote? Landholders only? "Men only" was a given in those days, sadly enough. Ultimately, our Founding Fathers decided to trust the people to vote the right candidates into office.

Most of our politicians and bureaucrats mean well, but the process of voting is so cumbersome that many people I have spoken to do not want to vote, or don't have the stamina and motivation to find voter registration forms, fill them out, and actually register to vote. They also do not trust the process, and feel their vote won't make any difference. In some cases this is true, as there are voting districts that have been politically manipulated so that one or another of the political parties have zero chance of winning.

This process is called gerrymandering, and involves re-drawing the boundaries of an electoral district to favor one party or class of people. The term has been around for a long time, and goes way back into the early nineteenth century. In 1812, the *Boston Gazette* coined the word as a tongue-in-cheek response to Massachusetts's governor (and Declaration of Independence signer) Elbridge Gerry's redistricting of the Boston area. The new district was awkwardly drawn to benefit his political party and just happened to look, on a map, like a salamander. Hence, gerry-mander. It's interesting how we develop words, isn't it?

Today, each state in America is allowed a certain number of congressional districts. The specific number of districts is based on population results from the US Census, which is done every ten years. But here's the kicker. The way those congressional districts are drawn is up to state legislatures. And since state legislatures are made up of politicians, the process can become quite political. If a legislature becomes mostly Republican or Democratic, one or another of the parties might gerrymander certain districts so their candidates can win more elections.

Possibly the first example of gerrymandering happened long before the term had ever been coined—and it involved several of our Founding Fathers. Late in 1788, just after Virginia voted to ratify the Constitution and join the union, former Governor Patrick Henry persuaded the Virginia state legislature to re-draw the 5th Congressional District. This forced Henry's biggest political enemy, James Madison, to run in the same district as the formidable James Monroe and hopefully lose. The plot failed, however, and Madison won. Eventually he became our fourth president. Monroe, of course, became the fifth leader of our nation.

Gerrymandering aside, the size, shape, and location of our congressional districts do not matter if people do not turn out to vote. The fact is, the number of people who are eligible to vote compared to those who actually do, is staggeringly low. Low enough that our current president floated the idea of a mandatory vote, as they do in Australia and Belgium. The *Washington Post* recently printed that, at 34.6 percent, 2014 voter turnouts for our midterm elections were the lowest since WWII, when many of our men were fighting overseas and did not have the opportunity to vote.

Voting is important, as it corrects our political pendulum swing. It also directs the will of the people. With 34 percent turnout, roughly one third of the voters make important electorate decisions for everyone. This means our elected officials might not be the candidates the majority of our citizens want to represent them.

We desperately need all eligible Americans in the voting booths, particularly our younger generation. Everyone needs to jump in to give their opinion of the candidates who are running for every office, not just major races, such as senatorial and presidential.

Voting in local races is important, too, as that is where the groundswell of opinion starts. School board elections, planning commissions, county commissioners, and small town mayoral races are some of the least supported by voters, but many elected to those offices go on to bigger and better things.

Former Alaskan Governor Sarah Palin was first elected mayor of tiny Wasilla, Alaska before she took the state's top job and eventually ran for vice-president of the United States on the John McCain ticket.

Another example is Jesse Ventura. Before he became governor of Minnesota, he was first elected as mayor of Brooklyn Park, a Minneapolis suburb. When he won the governorship as an independent, CBS news anchorman Dan Rather said, "The people of Washington [DC] could not be more surprised if Fidel Castro came loping across the Midwestern prairie on the back of a hippopotamus." Washingtonians may have been surprised, however the people of Minnesota were not. They had banded together to direct their will through the power of the vote.

The people of Washington [DC] could not be more surprised if Fidel Castro came loping across the Midwestern prairie on the back of a hippopotamus.

Other elections have been decided by a remarkably small margin, which means every vote really does count. As early as 1910, in an election for a congressional district in Buffalo, New York, challenger Charles Smith beat incumbent De Alva Alexander by just a few votes.

Of course, many remember the 2000 Presidential Race between Al Gore and George W. Bush. Bush defeated Gore by 537 votes in the state of Florida to win the election. Had Al Gore been able to get another six hundred people to the voting booths, people who supported him but didn't bother to vote, American history would have been changed forever.

Then there is one of our country's more bizarre elections. In the 1994 race for the Wyoming House of Representatives, Randall Luthi and Larry Call each finished with 1,941 votes. After a recount delivered the same numbers, Wyoming Governor Mike Sullivan settled the election in an unusual (but state-approved) fashion by drawing a ping-pong ball out of his cowboy hat. The ball with Luthi's name on it was drawn, and he was declared the winner.

Yes. Your vote counts, and so do the votes of your friends, family, co-workers, and neighbors. Our very low voter turnouts show that we have more people who complain about what is happening here in the United States, than people who vote. We need to change that, and that change starts with you. Get yourself and everyone you know into the voting booths.

Your vote counts, and so do the votes of your friends, family, co-workers, and neighbors.

On the other hand, many other people feel elected officials, contrary to the wishes of our Founding Fathers, represent *only* their own interests, rather than those of the constituency that elected them. In my opinion, sadly, they are often right. However, this feeling, should not keep people from voting. Through our collective votes, we have the power to change things we do not like about our cities, counties, states, and even our nation. We also have the power to keep in office those we feel are doing a good job in representing us. Former president Franklin Delano Roosevelt once said. "Democracy cannot succeed unless those who express their choice are prepared to choose wisely." I agree wholeheartedly.

Voting is also an essential element of our democratic, open, and free society. Two thoughts from Founding Father James Madison highlight the necessity for every citizen to vote. The first is, "All men having power ought to be distrusted to a certain degree." And then there is the second thought: "All power in human hands is liable to be abused." Our votes limit that power, and its abuse. Imperfect a system as it is, we all need to vote.

The good news is that help with our voting issues is on its way. Every day our best and brightest develop new technological solutions that limit glitches in the voting booth, provide secure backup systems, limit fraud, standardize the process across all voting locations, and ease the process for voters.

That little chad issue in Florida during the Bush/Gore presidential election would not have happened if Florida had modern voting machines. Their old machines still produced chads, punched holes in paper cards, to determine a voter's wishes. The entire election and the future of our country revolved around a few "hanging chads," or chads that were not cleanly punched. That is one reason why we desperately need to simplify, modernize, and standardize the voting process throughout our country.

Maybe some of the bright kids we will now educate with the trillions of dollars we save by staying out of bad neighborhoods could even develop a privatized system that will securely execute our voting process, and do it more efficiently. I am sure that a private enterprise voting system would cost the taxpayers far less than what the inefficient government is spending today—and be more effective.

I recently heard about a thirty-year-old tech guru who sold the brain-child of his twenties for multi-millions of dollars. His new pet project is "PlaceAVote," which is a voting app processed through your hand held device. His is a brilliant idea, and perfect for the millennial generation who were born and raised with a mobile device in their hands. His phone app also reveals how each and every public figure has voted, and what legislation he or she supports. Genius.

We live in the age of information, and an app such as this would solve the 8 percent turnout problem, once the issues of fraud prevention, double voting, etcetera, are firmly resolved. Other innovative ideas abound as well, and it will be interesting to see which of them take hold and are adopted into our voting procedures.

It is my hope that within the next decade we will have these issues solved. In the meantime, vote your conscience. Get to the polls and show up on election day. The only way to vote into office the candidates that are supported by the majority of citizens, candidates that are supported by *you*, is to cast your vote.

AMERICA'S SIMPLE SOLUTIONS

Let's consider the idea of a mandatory vote, as they do in Australia and Belgium. Only when a true majority of the people vote will we be sure that we have elected the most popular candidate into office.

We desperately need to simplify, modernize, and standardize the voting process throughout our country. Let's get our best and brightest on this today.

Remember that the people (you) have the power to reform, alter, or totally change the government, not the other way around. Vote, vote, vote. It is your right.

11

Environment

*Preservation of our environment is not a liberal or
conservative challenge; it's common sense.*
—Ronald Reagan, State of the Union address, Jan. 25, 1984

WHEN I WAS IN COLLEGE AT USC, I was an English major. Basically I read, and I read a lot. I found that reading literature, and just about whatever else struck my fancy, was an excellent way of educating myself. At top English universities in the nineteenth and early twentieth century students were said to be "reading history," or "reading economics" and the idea of reading was that was how you educated yourself. But to get a degree at USC in liberal arts, I couldn't just read. I had to take science as well. I was never stellar in chemistry, physics, or biology, so for my science requirement I chose geology.

Dr. Stone, (yes, his name really was Stone!) taught historic geology and it was a killer class about the history of our planet from a geological perspective. We learned that the history of the globe across the eras was best represented in the Grand Canyon, where the chronology of the earth was visible to all. I learned that certain animals appeared and then eventually disappeared. There was an Age of Amphibians, and one of dinosaurs, and in the early eras, there were trilobites that were big swimming bugs that evolved and changed over time. I found the whole thing fascinating.

One thing that was blatantly evident to me, as well as to any student of historical geology, was that the climate of the earth is in constant change, and that plants and animals appeared and disappeared according to that climate change. If it became colder, for example, the elephants of that time grew a warm coat of hair. Either that, or they died out. Climate change is the standard way of being for our earth, not the exception.

That means that global warming (hotter summers and colder winters), prolonged drought, and/or deluges of rain are normal and natural occurrences that have been going on since time began. However, the question of human disregard for our planet, destruction of our forests and animal kingdoms for commercial purposes, and use of our oceans as a human sewer is a whole different ball of wax. It is unquestionable that there are pollutants that mankind is carelessly putting into the environment, and this human pollution and destruction of our environment must be stopped, or limited to the very least possible. Together, this means that global warming and human pollution are two different subjects that should be examined separately.

Global warming and human pollution are two different subjects that should be examined separately.

Equally, the human race is a part of ecology, and our survival is an element of paramount importance to human ecology. The world should be considered and viewed with these glasses on as well. There are countless examples of human pollution and two things are for sure: 1) reckless burning of fossil fuel in smoke stacks near high-density population areas makes horrible air to breathe, and 2) dirty, polluted air is not healthful to humans. The world leader in this problem is definitely China. Some days in Beijing, the air is actually a thick brown, and many wear some kind of anti-pollution mask.

To illustrate the terrible air quality in China, researchers from Berkeley Earth, along with an international air quality-monitoring organization called AQICN.org found that air pollution in China kills about four thousand people every day, and accounts for about 17 percent of all deaths in the country. This is an extreme situation and it is ridiculous that the Chinese government has allowed this to happen. But, while the air pollution in China is severe, the World Health Organization has indicated that some areas of countries such as Iran, India, and Pakistan may be even worse off.

The Chinese, however, have realized the problem and are taking steps to correct it. Recently, on a trip to Beijing, I actually saw blue sky! My point is that climate change is an ongoing process and is normal. Pollution is not. But, sometimes a temporary, slight level of pollution is a necessary trade off to our increasing human needs as part of the world ecological system, which as I have mentioned already, also includes the human race. In these instances, allowing contamination of our environment should be studied rationally, and must be decided and reviewed on a case-by-case basis. We don't need hysterical or irrational decisions that any and all pollutants are horrible to the overall well-being of the human race.

Here's a simple example. Centuries ago, much of America was a vast plain where millions of buffalo roamed. Would it have been better not to populate the Midwest or the western states of the United States at all, due to fear of destroying the habitat of the American buffalo? Of course, that is what eventually did happen. But, it was done to make room for human populations to live, ranches to raise cattle, and farmers to raise crops to feed and create the new American nation.

Was it a bad idea to populate these areas? No, however the way the early Americans went about it was wrong. Passengers on transcontinental railroads used to have target practice by randomly killing buffalo. That is just gross. Mass killings of buffalo for sport, and then not even making use of their meat, bones, or hide was a horrid waste. And, failure to set aside large areas of land for buffalo and other game preserves was clearly short sighted.

It comes down to the way we undertake progress, and how we combine that progress with the respect and care of our environment. The fact is, once our natural resources are gone, they are gone. And once our pollution levels reach a certain tipping point, there will be no going back and our earth will slowly die. We need, once again, common sense.

It might be, though, that we don't need to become hysterical and halt all progress just because the earth's climate is changing. The climate has always changed. But, the reduction and elimination of pollution for the benefit of human health and the very survival of the human race is another matter. We all get the argument, now let's put it into a modern context; let's look at what a *National Geographic* expert has to say about saving the world's biggest cats:

> "Fifty percent of our oxygen comes from forests; the other from our oceans, 75 percent of all fresh water in one way comes from the forests. So the air we breathe and the water we drink comes from the homes of these precious animals.
>
> "If we save the forests of the world like the Amazon for the jaguar and puma, central African forests for lions, leopards and elephants, the forests of India and south east Asia for the tiger, we help to save ourselves."
>
> —From an article in *The Dodo, Nat Geo Explorer* by Dr. Jane Goodall

Let's apply this kind of reasonable, common sense thinking to actual environmental situations of today. In the argument of environment versus progress, and supposing that the US economy was in a position to afford a revamp of our antiquated train system, we could construct a high-speed public train transportation system such as that of Japan (who built theirs in 1964), France, or China. This would also be a partial answer to our decaying roads and infrastructure. With more people traveling by train, and fewer by car, our roads would need less maintenance.

The fact is that each little town and county that a proposed high speed train needs to cross has some environmental law or regulation that ties up the high speed train plan by months, or even years. These delays can cost US taxpayers hundreds of millions of dollars. In addition, another problem exists because the proposed train might be scheduled to cross a marsh land where the "blue winged spider" or some other obtuse insect or animal known to man lives. Of course that particular species is on our government's endangered species list.

There are solutions. One is to transplant the endangered "blue winged spider" to a similar habitat that is safely away from the train track. Certainly that would cost less than running the train miles away from the marsh. And with all due respect to my fictitious "blue winged spider," there are many thousands of species that disappear and appear at any moment in time—all without human help.

Sadly, I fear more are disappearing due to mankind than appearing, but there needs to be an intelligent, case-by-case balance between environmental protection and economic progress. Sometimes, it might be that we need to choose the lesser of two evils, and find the least environmentally disruptive solution. The ultimate goal in an ideal world would be to eliminate pollution completely as our technology progresses.

There needs to be an intelligent, case-by-case balance between environmental protection and economic progress.

Here's a question for you. Would we rather have a society where our children are properly educated, where the homeless are off the streets, where the truly needy are cared for, and where we are not dependent on oil from a "bad neighborhood" that costs us trillions through our participation in religious wars? Or, would we rather preserve the marshland of the "blue winged spider?" Of course, we want both. But, it just might be that we have to make compromises and trade offs to get them. We do need to remain sensitive to our environment, but I will choose to educate my children over preserving a little known species of spider that may be able to be relocated. These are questions that surface when there is an oil pipeline being proposed, or when off shore drilling is a question, or a company is exploring for oil near a sedimentary rock formation.

A number of other environmental issues are on the forefront of the progress versus environmental preservation discussion. One is certainly fracking. Fracking is a relatively new form of oil drilling that pumps water into underground shale formations allowing the oil to rise to the top. In the world of thirty-dollar (or higher) barrels of oil, high consumer demand, a perceived oil shortage, and low interest rates, fracking pushed America past Saudi Arabia as the largest oil producer in the world in May of 2014. Fracking has been banned in many places globally, and has sometimes been labeled as a pollutant or a potential pollutant of ground water. But in North Dakota, Texas, Oklahoma, and Louisiana it was and is the engine of boom times, especially when oil was skyrocketing to far above one hundred dollars a barrel.

Others have argued that the fracking process might pollute only in the immediate area surrounding the fracking wells, or maybe not at all. We still don't know, as this technology is very new. The fact is, we are not yet sure that fracking is such a horrible pollutant as some have argued. USAToday reported in September of 2014 that a study that included researchers from Duke, Stanford, and Dartmouth Universities, and the University of Rochester, found that faulty wells, not fracking, was the main reason for contamination of wells and drinking water in parts of Texas and Pennsylvania. If fracking does pollute, and it certainly might, I am convinced that American ingenuity can solve this problem—if our government leaves the private sector alone long enough to figure it out.

Some also think fracking causes earthquakes—and it could. In July of 2015, the state of Oklahoma experienced a record forty earthquakes in one week and in the past few years has more than doubled their annual number of quakes. Oklahoma Governor Mary Fallin has acknowledged that the link between these earthquake and fracking is not the fracking itself, but due to the wastewater disposal procedures used in the process. CNBC also reported in June of 2015 that scientists at Stanford University found that earthquakes near oil drilling operations were not caused by the drilling or fracking, but by those operations' disposal of waste water in deep rock formations. We need to come up with a wastewater disposal system that is less environmentally harmful.

We all must continually be vigilant about getting the real facts, and not mindlessly adapting a particular point of view. Both liberal and conservative blocks are guilty of adapting certain view points and "jumping on the bandwagon" as a result of false information.

To me, fracking is a perfect example in this debate, and where, on occasion, you have to take a risk. It might be a temporary risk, and maybe it is the best of two mediocre options, but it is a risk all the same. In this case the choice would be between the following. A: for America to have a presence in the Middle East, and spend trillions of dollars on the religious war there because "it is in our interest" due to our need for oil. Or B: potentially damage a limited amount of farmland, frack for oil, become oil self-sufficient, and save trillions of dollars from the military "war business." This money can then be put into education, rebuilding our infrastructures and transport systems, and once again making America strong and a beacon of hope for the world. If it were up to me, I would take that environmental risk and choose the latter. How about you?

If it is later proven, without a doubt and contrary to the facts as we know them today, that major damage is being done to groundwater and no solutions are possible, then we should cross that bridge when we get there. But for the moment, the environmental trade off for our betterment is necessary. Plus, getting rid of dependency on Middle Eastern oil will help transform America to a substantially better place for our children. We owe that to them. This is nuts and bolts common sense business. Sadly, US government isn't run that way.

Another environmental issue at the forefront is the massive slaughter of African wild animals through poaching for "medicinal" needs and the ornamental desires of the growing Chinese middle class. This illegal trade in animal body parts is due to ignorance and lack of education, and it would be a terrible tragedy if the ecosystem of the continent of Africa continues to be irrevocably damaged by these mass killings. Close to one hundred thousand elephants have been slaughtered there for the illegal ivory trade in the past three years. And, rapidly disappearing rhinos are savagely attacked and killed by poachers in helicopters. This, all to cut off their horns to send to China to be used as a homeopathic Viagra substitute.

The root cause of these atrocities, besides the ignorance of the Chinese *nouveau riche*, the newly rich Chinese, is closely related to abject poverty in Africa. These poachers are paid well for the wild animal body parts. The problem also relates to a lack of will on the part of the international community to assist, educate, and give tools of betterment to impoverished African communities that are found next to our last remaining wild lands and game reserves. These people should be educated to understand that it is in their best interests to preserve wildlife.

Let's pretend the African bush and forests were off limits to poachers and left in pristine condition. We can use Botswana in our example, as even today it is truly teaming with wildlife. Botswana is also visited annually by thousands of wildlife tourists They have a multimillion-dollar global tourist industry that has far more value than poaching, and is highly beneficial to the indigenous population. This is the supply side of the equation.

On the demand side in China, the international community must turn up the volume, and I mean *really* turn up the volume, to curtail the illegal trade of these animal body parts. In my travels in China, I have seen huge stores filled *only* with ivory artifacts, whose value increases regularly due to the huge demand for them. Compounding the situation is that the ivory trade is half-heartedly controlled, and that the Chinese consider ivory artifacts as an "investment." If the Chinese government can stop their population from criticizing them, and from having babies, surely they can clamp down on the trade of material objects, just as the rest of the world has done already.

Why does the preservation of wildlife matter to Americans? The World Wildlife Foundation reports that forests, particularly rainforests, are home to 80 percent of the world's biodiversity. Forests also play a critical role in slowing climate change because they soak up carbon dioxide and other greenhouse gases that would otherwise be floating around in our atmosphere and contribute to ongoing changes in climate patterns.

There is no question that forests and habitats of animals are intimately tied together with human life. Our world is one large ecosystem, one globe, and the rapid disappearance of any major species is an event important to all living beings.

It is obvious that we have innumerable environmental issues here in the US and abroad. And that's the thing about the environment. It is global and knows no borders. That which happens in the Far East can affect us here in the United States. That's why we need to approach these issues with a cool and objective eye. We see over and over that long-winded, wordy government regulations end up stifling progress and do not have the desired impact on the environmental problem being addressed. Here's my simple solution, and it involves human nature: let's get the private sector involved and make it highly beneficial and financially profitable to clean up the environment and solve our environmental problems.

A recent article in the *International New York Times* about the annual Danish-based INDEX Awards spoke of an award given to a twenty-one-year-old Dutch engineering student named Boyan Slat, who designed an inexpensive way of solving one of the world's biggest environmental problems: cleaning up the plastic trash that is polluting our oceans. The proposed solution was called The Ocean Cleanup Array and Slat was awarded one hundred thousand dollars of the $580,000 prize money that was allotted to the top five entries.

His proposed solution is to start a two-year test in the water near Tsushima, an island in the Korean Strait between Japan and Korea. Financed by $2.2 million of crowd-funding, the test will construct a two-thousand-meter long barrier, the world's largest floating structure, at the center of one of the circular currents where plastic debris has congregated to form a gigantic "garbage patch."

After being collected, the plastic will be removed, shipped to dry land, and be recycled. Powered by energy generated from the sun and waves, the system promises to provide a faster, cheaper, and less destructive means than any existing method of clearing the plastic junk that kills as many as one hundred thousand birds, fish, and other marine creatures *every day*. If the test goes well, this system could be set up in similar circular currents around the world. And the income from recycling could make a partial payment toward the cost of undertaking this process.

Wow, what a great idea! This is a prime example of educating our younger generations, giving them the tools to think, and then the freedom to find solutions. If we enhance personal freedom, rather than curtail it, there will be a legion of young Boyan Slat's who find environmental and other solutions to our problems, while creating jobs at the same time.

When it comes to electric cars and trucks, we need to develop and support these industries, and we need to drive zero pollution electric automobiles. These are choices each of us can make, and if the batteries of these cars are the only pollutants, don't ban electric cars because they have battery pollutants, let's find some American ingenuity and develop batteries that don't pollute.

It is also good to note that the environment does not just mean rural landscapes. The word also covers the environment in our cities. The air quality and the streets of our cities both need to be cleaned up, and our parks need a great deal of attention. In Los Angeles, when exiting the Pasadena Freeway there are a series of tunnels from the 1940s that have beautiful white tile on the lower part of the walls. These tiles have not been industrially washed in years. If they were cleaned and maintained, it would lighten the tunnels, make objects inside the tunnels (such as other cars) more visible, and improve our city environment.

Why not give welfare recipients training in city maintenance, rather than free money? Among many other jobs, those in Los Angeles could clean the tunnels and other areas of the city. This would give people a sense of pride in a job well done, and improve the city environment in the process. This solution is used in Japan today, and as you travel the streets of the metropolises there, you see welfare recipients working as gardeners, street cleaners, and other city maintenance jobs while waiting for the perfect position to open up and match their skill set Welfare recipients in Japan are *not* idle at home watching TV and collecting money for doing nothing. In time, these former welfare recipients will rejoin the work force with a new set of skills. In life, and in the working environment, I find that one thing often leads to another. Pick up new tools and make things happen. We just have to start.

AMERICA'S SIMPLE SOLUTIONS

Preservation of our environment is not a liberal or conservative challenge; it's common sense. Our Native Americans had the right idea in understanding they needed to leave their individual environments cleaner than when they arrived in that space.

Let's build high-speed public train transportation systems. This would also be a partial answer to our decaying roads and infrastructure. With more people traveling by train, and fewer by car, our roads would need less maintenance and we add less air pollution into our environment.

When it comes to fracking, we must come up with a wastewater disposal system that is less environmentally harmful.

When it comes to environmental issues, we must be continually vigilant about getting the real facts, and not mindlessly adapt a liberal or conservative point of view.

Many of the people in our private sector are really smart. Let's get them involved and make it highly beneficial and financially profitable for them to clean up the environment and solve our environmental problems.

Opt to drive the least polluting automobile that you can. Ideally, we all need to drive zero pollution electric automobiles.

Whenever possible, rather than "free" money, give welfare recipients jobs that keep our communities clean and litter free.

12

Welfare, Social Security, and Entitlements

Government giveaway programs destroy the human spirit.
—Franklin Delano Roosevelt

THIS CHAPTER COULD HAVE BEEN DIVIDED INTO three different chapters, but because this trio of topics are so closely intertwined, they have stayed together. To be quite clear, and not allow any misinterpretation of this chapter, we definitely need to take care of people who, through no fault of their own, cannot provide for themselves. It is the responsibility of any educated, advanced, and enlightened society to care for people who are truly needy. This group might include, but is not limited to, people who are elderly, disabled, mentally challenged, or critically ill. Children without parents or caretakers, those who are dying, people who have been displaced through no fault of their own, those temporarily out of a job not due to their own volition, and those who have been struck by the tragedy of natural disaster also fall into this category.

It is the responsibility of any educated, advanced, and enlightened society to care for people who are truly needy.

According to Census.gov, the 2010 US census revealed that the number of "truly needy" in our country is between 10 and 13 percent of the population as a whole. As noted earlier, President Reagan thought the number could be roughly 10 percent of the population, and insisted that those who were truly needy be cared for. Reagan may have been right on with his numbers during the time he was president, but our aging population insures that the number of people with severe needs is growing, as Census.gov reports that in the eighty-year-old and over population group, 71 percent of people have a severe disability. A severe disability is one that makes it difficult for a person to perform day-to-day activities such as dressing, eating, bathing, or other self-care tasks.

Equally as definite as the fact that we need to care for the needy, is that there should never be open-ended welfare programs that invite generation after generation of potentially productive people to remain dependent on government charity. Such charity deprives able-bodied people of the incentive to work, and requires productive people to support those who are physically and mentally able to have a job. Ongoing welfare prolongs an endless cycle of dependency that robs men and women of their dignity, and an ability to find personal happiness and satisfaction in their valuable lives. We've already discussed that productive people are generally happy and have a positive outlook on life. That's another reason that open-ended welfare is a waste of our nation's most valuable assets: our people, and their participation and creativity toward a better America.

Any adult who has the ability to work, who has the mental capacity to learn a skill or a trade, should not be classified as truly needy. Nor should those individuals who refuse to work, or refuse to make a positive contribution to their own well-being and happiness, or that of the society in which they live.

How many people are we talking about? A 2015 Census.gov report shows that approximately 52.2 million (or 21.3 percent) of the population receives some form of government assistance or subsidy. This includes:

50 percent of female-led households

41.6 percent of black Americans

39.2 percent of children

37.3 percent of those who did not graduate from high school

36.4 percent of Hispanics

16.6 percent of people age 18 to 64

13.2 percent of whites

12.6 percent of people age 65 and older

It is easy to wonder, of those percentages, how many of the people fall into the "truly needy" category. Yes, some of the people who receive supportive benefits are working, but not earning a "living wage." Some have a partial disability and are only able to work part time. I get that, but there are many who could work, and do not. Specific numbers are hard to find and vary widely from source to source, but a quick search on the Internet delivers numerous examples of criminal convictions for food stamp, Medicare, and other types of fraud. How many other people are still getting away with it?

Sadly, ours is a system full of individuals who take advantage of honest, taxpaying citizens. It is an unjust system that has become out of control, and we should demand an immediate correction. The future of the American nation depends on it. On August 9, 2013, the Cato Institute, an American think tank in Washington, DC, released a paper titled "The Work versus Welfare Trade-Off." In it they reported that in the eight most generous states, benefits can be equivalent to a $20 wage, which far exceeds any minimum wage.

Let's look at this more closely, and examine some of the misconceptions that brought about our sad state of affairs. Let's also look at what other highly-educated societies have successfully done to avoid the situation we now have. We must take any opportunity we can to learn how to reverse our course.

Again, it's imperative to look to our Founding Fathers for guidance on the role of our government. James Madison was prolific on the subject, and said, "Charity is no part of the legislative duty of the government."

He also said, "I cannot undertake to lay my finger on that article of the Constitution which granted a right to Congress of expending, on objects of benevolence, the money of their constituents."

Then, to use the words of FDR, an ongoing welfare program "destroys the human spirit."

These are just a few of the many remarks and observations made by a wide array of our former leaders on redistributing the wealth of the nation from one citizen to another, commonly known as welfare. But, contrary to the vision and intentions of our Founding Fathers, one of the primary roles of the US and state governments today is the redistribution of wealth. This is rather than support the creation of new wealth by freedom-loving citizens. Plus, our government is progressively assuming an increasing role in determining what percentage of a taxpayer's labors must annually be transferred to a fellow citizen(s). This is done through excessive taxation and stringent regulations on individuals and companies, all under the guise of welfare.

On a personal level I have come across numerous instances of welfare abuse. Just in my own circle of friends I learned of a cousin of a friend who lives here in California. No member of the cousin's family has worked much, if at all, during the past ten or more years. They live in a modest home, go out to dinner several times each week, and go to the movies several times a month with their entire family. Living on welfare, their time is their own. If they run short of cash, they pick up a bit of under the table work from time to time. Life is not bad on the government dole. Unfortunately, instances such as these abound.

It is a way of life, but a way of life that must end if we are going to turn this great country around. It undermines the family. As it stands, sometimes it is better financially for the family if the dad walks out. If he stayed they wouldn't get a welfare check. That's wrong. Dads should be encouraged to stay. Teenage girls who get pregnant get a welfare check that allows them to get their own apartment, and move out and away from parental guidance at an immature age. Then they discover they can increase their monthly welfare check by simply getting pregnant again. That's wrong, too. Remember our chapter about family, and the importance of family to so many aspects of a successful society and a successful America? Long term and extended welfare generally is detrimental to the family.

There are three important things to recognize in our endeavor to stop welfare abuse. (Two of the items are important in getting people who don't belong on welfare off of it, and in returning to them their most precious gift: human dignity.) First, we absolutely must tighten eligibility standards. And second, we must eliminate loopholes. We need to openly recognize these two impediments and find solutions. To keep raising taxes on "the rich" to unproductively pour more money into a bucket full of holes is no solution. All it does is perpetuate welfare abuse.

The third impediment to ending welfare abuse is the welfare bureaucracy itself, as it is self-protecting and self-perpetuating. Most government employees will do all they can to perpetuate their jobs and keep their income. If welfare expands, then there is more work and more job security.

One solution is to be vigilant and attack fraud with economic sanctions on lawyers who encourage false claims, as well as on those who file false claims. Another solution goes back to the concept of family. In other countries, families help and support family members much more than we do here. We need families to take better care of their own. We can also provide more day care for low-income families so moms and dads can work. We can encourage kids to stay in school so they can become educated enough to earn a living wage. The entrepreneur also needs to be encouraged, not discouraged, and businesses and government need to eliminate the twenty-year pension. If someone goes to work at age twenty, he can retire at forty? What is right about that?

So what do other countries do? Recently, I had a conversation with a dear Swiss friend, Andre Karlen. Andre was a full judge at age thirty, which is unheard of in stodgy Switzerland. He is also one of the most brilliant people I know. We were together as students at the University of Madrid in the 1960s and traveled throughout Europe together staying in hostels. He is multi-lingual, a Swiss lawyer besides being a judge, and recently participated in rewriting the constitution of the Canton of Valais in southern Switzerland. Andre has always had a global perspective, and is a bright, kind man who relies on common sense.

I asked Andre what percentage of the Swiss population is on welfare and he answered that it was in the low single digits. As I recall, he said it was roughly 3 percent. Andre also pointed out that in Switzerland people cannot stay on welfare very long, certainly not nearly as long as the United States average of three to four years. I remember him mentioning a period of two years. After that the welfare checks begin to decline in value until they are reduced to zero.

I asked Andre how the Swiss system worked, and he told me that their welfare office categorizes the candidate who requests welfare as a "work seeker." When the person first applies, they evaluate his or her situation fully. What skills do they have? What has the work experience been? What education and background is there? What skills can be learned? If necessary, the Swiss assist the candidate in learning new skills that are needed in the Swiss economy.

Once the evaluation is made, the "work seeker" is offered a job, either with the government, or in the private sector. This initial job might not be perfect. It must be within a certain radius of the candidate's home residence, but it gets him back working and in the productive work force. The Swiss know that one thing leads to another and that it is important to re-enter the work force as quickly as possible. The Swiss also feel it is important to be productive, even if it is a job that is below the level or qualifications of the candidate. Just get the person working.

The "work seeker" can reject two job proposals, but if the third proposal is rejected, he or she is then reclassified as a "work refuser." Welfare checks are then reduced over time, and if he or she refuses to accept any job, they eventually are paid zero by the Swiss welfare system. That's it. This system works, and has to be billions of dollars cheaper than the welfare abuse system that we now operate.

The Swiss also feel it is important to be productive, even if it is a job that is below the level or qualifications of the candidate. Just get the person working.

We need to get busy, today, and get private enterprise to help America implement a solution similar to this. Welfare in America must be immediately reformed. If the Swiss solution is not perfect for America, then let's look at all the welfare systems of the advanced industrial nations throughout the world. Let's take what works and what is good in each system, and start the process to reform our dysfunctional method of caring for our truly needy in a manner that is just to all citizens. Let's also remember equally as much the efforts of those who work and support the existence of our welfare through their payment of taxes.

We have to get America working. We can do this by setting reform goals, just as we do in private enterprise, then let's meet the goals, and execute and implement the reforms. We simply can't afford to keep doing what we are doing. Let's also listen to the founder of our welfare system, Franklin Delano Roosevelt who suggested long-term recipients get off the "welfare narcotic."

▲

This leads us to our next subject, Social Security, which is another disaster headed for insolvency. But, it doesn't need to be if we stop, take a step back, use our common sense, and implement logical solutions.

Social Security is something we all should strongly support. The concept of Social Security is logical, humanitarian, and an essential element for the well-being of any enlightened and educated society. But immediate improvements are needed, and Social Security *must* be reformed now. If not, it will either go bankrupt, or the government will print so much worthless paper money that recipients will get the money they were promised, but the money won't represent a monetary value sufficient for living out a retirement.

Certainly, it will not be a payback to the worker in equivalent value of the money that was deducted from his paycheck during his entire working life. The Social Security recipient will receive, for example, the twenty-three hundred dollars a month he was promised, except the twenty-three hundred will only pay his rent, or his groceries. Or, it will cover a fraction of what it should under a forced inflation of the US dollar, which is something that will have to happen if we do not implement changes immediately.

Here is something that Americans have been deceived about for years. Americans for many years have been told that we all contribute to an old age insurance fund that is set aside for our retirement years. In fact, Ronald Reagan told us in his book, An American Life, that there is no "fund" at all. He wrote that the Social Security deduction from every American's paycheck is a tax producing revenue stream that Congress has used for a number of purposes. These purposes include offering "needy" citizens entitlements, while letting reserves that should benefit those who have paid their hard earned money into Social Security fall into a black hole of government debt. As Reagan says, this is a bit different than what we all were taught in civics in middle school or junior high, and certainly was not the intention of the original Social Security Act. That was passed at the height of the Depression in 1935, was enacted into law in 1937, and the first benefits were paid out in 1940.

Ronald Reagan told us in his book, *An American Life*, that there is no "fund" at all.

The world in 1935 when Social Security was initiated was indeed different from today. Life expectancy was lower. People smoked, automobile and air travel were less safe, and medicine was far less advanced. For example, penicillin wasn't used on human patients until 1942, seven years after Social Security was enacted. Exercise had also not yet been proven to be an essential element to longevity.

Today life expectancy is longer, people are healthier, and they know that continuing productive work into one's late years increases longevity. At the driving range where I practice, Nick, the maintenance guy, is ninety-four and works like a fifty-year-old. The number of people living to be one hundred years of age has skyrocketed.

Recently, on the cover of *Time* magazine, there was an image of a baby, and the subtitle was that this young person was going to live to be

140 years old. I myself have every intention of living productively and actively until I am at least 120 years old. I have four-year-old twins, my boy Iggy, and my little lady, Chloe. I have every intention of walking Chloe down the aisle and giving her to her future husband. I hope she doesn't make the youthful mistake I made and get married too young. To me, thirty is a fine age to marry, so I would be ninety-six when I walk with her down the aisle. My point is that life expectancy is rapidly on the rise—and will continue to increase.

Let's assume the following scenario: that there will be no change in the spending habits of Congress, and that Congress will continue with their addiction to debt and spend far more revenue than they collect. Indeed, Congress seems to make no attempt to reduce the national debt, which today stands at about 19 trillion dollars. For baby boomers, that generation of people born between 1946 and 1964, to collect the Social Security that they are owed, there must be an even larger, younger group that is paying into Social Security. That is not the case, so something's gotta give. We can't just put our head in a hole and hope. If what is going on now continues, Social Security will declare insolvency in the early years of the 2030s. Some say it will happen even sooner. We need to change what we are doing.

We can't just put our head in a hole and hope.

America's simple solution: Immediately, we need to push the retirement age of Social Security to seventy-five. Today, the average American man lives to be seventy-eight years old, and American women, on average, live four years longer. Both life expectancies are increasing, and will continue to if people are kept productive. Pushing the retirement age to something that resembles a comparable retirement age from 1935 will delay the insolvency of Social Security, and allow the system time to regroup and reform the mess that was created by politicians who promised entitlements, which incidentally, got them elected. The insanity has to stop.

▲

On a different note, things that strike me when I travel are the various entitlements that are guaranteed by different governments around the world. The western world, especially Europe, seems to feel they are being enlightened and humanitarian by guaranteeing cradle to grave care and security as an entitlement for being a citizen of a certain country. Some of the rights assured throughout Europe (and the list is growing in the United States) are the right to:

Vote
Healthcare
Education
Work
A retirement pension sufficient to live your life in comfort
A passport and freedom to travel
Have and use public transportation
Own a home
A fair judicial system
Free speech
Freedom of religion
Work for ten months and get paid for thirteen. (In most of Europe workers have one month off in the summer, two weeks for a spring vacation, and two weeks either at Christmas or in the fall. All this adds up to ten months of work, but vacation time is paid, as well. Plus, many get an additional check for "vacation money," which is often the equivalent of a thirteenth month. All of this can cost the employer roughly double the worker's salary or hourly wage.)

That's just to name a few rights. In certain countries in Asia, people have the right to work, but it is their own responsibility to prepare themselves and find this work. That is their *only* right, the right to take care of themselves and their family. Because of the lack of entitlements, people have a great sense of personal accountability, pride of self progress, and that all important word "gratitude" is a big part of people's lives. People do not expect anything to be handed to them on a silver platter, and families take care of family members. No one expects anyone to provide for them. They must do it for themselves.

And as welfare increases in the west, what happens to our productivity? What happens to growth? Job creation? Entrepreneurship? "Larger welfare states are inimical [unfavorable] not only to growth but also to employment due to the tendency to raise the cost of labor and thereby decreasing employers ability to afford to employ more workers." (Political Science Professor Isabela Mares, Columbia University, New York City, 2007) Does this sound familiar?

Is it a wonder that most of the continent of Asia is in a state of ascent, and the western, entitled world is in a state of decline? It's easy to write yourself a check, or to elect a politician to gift you all kinds of entitlements. There is only one catch. There has to be money in the bank to cover the check. And right now, we don't have it.

To quote Reagan again: "Welfare's purpose should be to eliminate, as far as possible, the need for its own existence." What a wise, wise man he was.

AMERICA'S SIMPLE SOLUTIONS

Open-ended welfare is a waste of our nation's most valuable assets: our people, and their participation and creativity toward a better America. Let's use a system like they have in Switzerland and get people working.

We absolutely must tighten eligibility standards and can do this by taking an honest look at who needs welfare, and for how long.

We must eliminate loopholes in our welfare system. Right away, an independent council can make recommendations that we implement ASAP.

If lawyers encourage false claims and help facilitate them, let's tighten the penalties for these kinds of fraud. Let's make the penalties so stiff that any legal professional will think long and hard before acting.

For young parents with no family to care for and teach their children, our best and brightest teachers must be recruited into early childhood education so we can provide more quality day care for low-income families. Education must start early.

Every adult must take time to encourage kids to stay in school. Only then can our youth become educated enough to earn a living wage.

Entrepreneurs also need to be encouraged, not discouraged, and businesses and government need to eliminate the twenty-year pension. These pensions are too costly, and most of us are able to contribute productively to society for much longer than that.

Let's adopt the Swiss management of welfare and use their limited time frame and dwindling checks for those who do not accept offered jobs. (This for all except the needy who are truly disabled and cannot work.)

And, because we are all working longer, let's graduate in a new retirement age for Social Security to seventy-five. This will ease the strain on Social Security and give it a better chance of being around a while longer.

"The best place to find a helping hand is at the end of your own arm." —Chinese Proverb

13

Gender and Equality

Freedom cannot be achieved unless women have been emancipated from all forms of oppression. Our endeavors must be about the liberation of the woman, the emancipation of the man and the liberty of the child.
—Nelson Mandela, president, South Africa

I ADMIT THAT OVER THE YEARS I have been accused of being sexist. The reason is that over the many decades of owning businesses, I have hired more women into leadership positions than men. When it comes to me, it's men, of course, who use the term sexist.

When I fill a position in one of my companies, I have always looked for the best person for the job. Gender has never come into my decisions, but when I look at the qualifications of two or three of the best applicants, a woman is often the most qualified person, so I hire her. Some of that has to do with the fact that I am in the apparel business and there are traditionally more women interested in that field than men. However, many other fields employ more women than men, but men fill most of the leadership roles. This is the case with our US government.

In recent years as a nation we have made great strides toward equality in all areas. Whether it is gender, race, age, sexual orientation, or religion, we are far more equal than we were when our country was founded. But there is still a long way to go. To understand how far we have come, we must start near the beginning.

There is a story about John Adams when he went to Philadelphia in 1776 to work on the Declaration of Independence. Before he left, his wife, Abigail (a future First Lady), asked her husband to "remember the ladies." John must have either forgotten or dismissed his wife's request, because as we all know, our Declaration of Independence states: "We hold these truths to be self-evident, that all *men* are created equal."

The word "men" as used in that day and age could be considered an all-inclusive term for people or citizens, but in view of the times, it is probably a given that "men" indeed meant just that. And, because many states allowed slavery, our declaration probably meant that our Founding Fathers felt that only white males should be considered equal. Unfortunately, our Founding Fathers had little to say about gender, and equality has been an ongoing struggle for women in the United States ever since.

During the days of our early leaders, and for a century or more beyond that, a woman was considered to be the property of her husband—much like slaves were. Back then, women actually had no rights at all. They could not even have a bank account or own property, and this left them at the mercy of their man, or in the case of an unmarried woman, the senior male member of her household.

Unfortunately, our Founding Fathers had little to say about gender, and equality has been an ongoing struggle for women in the United States ever since.

Change came slowly. The 19th Amendment did not come along to legalize a woman's right to vote until 1920. Black men, on the other hand, had gained the right to vote as a result of the 15th Amendment a full fifty years earlier in 1870. Well, they had gained the right in theory, as they were subject to intimidation and punishment if they had the audacity to actually try to vote.

The Equal Pay Act, signed into law in 1963 by President John F. Kennedy, helped to ensure equal earnings for both men and women by making it illegal to discriminate based on sex. When the Equal Pay Act was signed, women earned roughly 59 cents to every man's dollar. That gap has lessened, but has not disappeared completely. Not yet, anyway.

The list of discriminations and inequality toward women goes on. As recently as 1965, married couples in Connecticut could not use contraceptives. In 1967 it was still legal to organize classified newspaper employment ads by gender, and until 1972 it was legal to discriminate against women's sports programs in schools. And, it wasn't until 1986 that sexual harassment was deemed a form of job discrimination.

We've talked of Ronald Reagan quite a bit, but he was breaking new ground when he said that one of the top three goals of his presidency would be to appoint a woman to the Supreme Court. This was a big deal, and somewhat controversial in 1981 when he first assumed office. He made good on that goal that same year, though, with his appointment of Sandra Day O'Connor. Since then three other women have also served on the high court.

No matter their race, ethnicity, age, occupation, religion, sexual orientation, or education, all women in the United States are still impacted by the gender wage gap.

No matter their race, ethnicity, age, occupation, religion, sexual orientation, or education, all women in the United States are still impacted by the gender wage gap. While we are improving as a nation, we are not nearly where we should be, nor are we even close to other world leaders. According to the Pew Research Center, and depending on the job category or specific industry, in 2013 women still earned, on average, about 84 cents for every dollar a man earns. Catalyist.org reports that in 2014 women earned 82.5 percent of men's salaries, compared to 62.1 percent in 1979.

At the current rate, it will take more than forty years (until 2058) for women and men to reach equal pay status. That means that the average, full-time working woman will lose more than $460,000 over a forty-year period in wages, due only to her gender. Nothing is right about that.

Many countries in Europe, including France, Germany, and Poland, passed laws guaranteeing equal pay for equal work in their constitutions before the foundation of the European Union (EU) in 1957. More recently, the World Economic Forum (WEF), a Swiss nonprofit committed to improving the state of the world, has done an annual Global Gender Gap Report, and the US is nowhere to be seen in the top ten countries. In fact, we sit at number twenty. The top countries out of the 142 that were analyzed are all Nordic nations, and include, in order: Iceland, Finland, Norway, Sweden, and Denmark.

Despite numerous tries, America could not even get the Equal Rights Amendment ratified.

The WEF's Global Gender Gap Report measures gender differences across the areas of health, education, economy, and politics. According to their findings in 2014 no country in the world has fully closed the gender gap yet, but all of the top five listed countries (Iceland, Finland, Norway, Sweden, and Denmark) have closed more than 80 percent of it. In the meantime, despite numerous tries, America could not even get the Equal Rights Amendment ratified.

As hard as it has been for women, they are not the only ones who suffer from gender discrimination, because gender equality is not just a women's issue. Men are discriminated against every day when it comes to issues such as family leave, parenting, and child custody, and that kind of discrimination weakens our families. A father who is ordered by our courts to see his children only every other weekend has a very hard time being an effective parent.

In fact, inequality of any sort is a negative blight on our nation. Here's what one of our former presidents had to say about gender discrimination.

Above: Dad and Mom on their wedding day with Uncle Joe, Rev. Joseph Vaughan, who performed the ceremony. One summer all six of us kids got the mumps and he came to San Rafael where we were staying for the summer and nursed our family back to health. We all loved him so much.

Left: Mom and Dad in May 1941.

PONY RIDE

Above: My brother Eric, me, and my sister Anne in 1949 or 1950. My youngest kids, Iggy and Chloe, love the Griffith Park pony ride, as much as I did more than sixty years ago.

Left: Top to bottom: older sister and brother Anne and Eric, me, and younger sister and brother Punky and Paul. I must have been about eight years old.

Left: I was too slow and pudgy to be good at baseball. Golf was my sport (and still is), as I didn't have to run.

Below: Sister Thomas OP, a Dominican nun; my dad's younger brother, Rev. Clyde Werts SJ (Jesuit) who was head of the engineering department at Loyola University in Playa del Rey; Rev. Richard Vaughan, my mother's younger brother who had a PhD in psychology, and later became the Provincial for the western half of the US for the Jesuit order. I don't recognize the other two nuns but I believe one is a cousin.

Left: Age seventeen. My high school graduation photo.

Below: My Dad and Mom, and her aunt, Virginia Lucille Werts, a Dominican nun and President of Dominican College in San Rafael, California, along with another nun. The photo was taken in Benicia, California in the mid-1940s.

Left: Florence, Italy, October 1972. I was proud to be a Dutch-based flower power entrepreneur.

Above: Ansterdam, 1971, with one of the sales girls in front of my first Salty Dog store on the Nieuwendijk, near the Amsterdam train station.

Below: My siblings and me as adults. L-R: Anne, mom of four and world traveler; Eric, a computer specialist in Silcon Valley; me; Punky, a career teacher; Paul, a financial analyst and stockbroker; and Carl, a dentist who studied at Georgetown.

Left: Me, Eric (who passed away from ALS), and Carl at our parents' fiftieth wedding anniversary in the mid 1990s at my home in the old Hollywood Hills. The home once belonged to Maurice Chevalier, the French entertainer, actor, and singer. The English Bulldog is "Fat."

Below: The American Rag store in Osaka, Japan opened in 2000.

Left: Close friend and golf coach Claude Harman with my wife Amanda and me in Dubai in 2010.

Above: At the flagship LaBrea store many years after I spent several days and nights defending it during the Rodney King riots.

Left: In Bangkok, Thailand in 2015 at American Rag Cie store.

Below: With sons Julian and Mark Olivier.

Left: My son-in-law Ike Pius with my daughter Zoey and my grandkids Ekena and Adora.

Below: Amanda and me with our twins, Iggy and Chloe.

Gender equality is not just a women's issue. Men are discriminated against every day when it comes to issues such as family leave, parenting, and child custody, and that kind of discrimination weakens our families.

"It is not women and girls alone who suffer. It damages all of us. The evidence shows that investing in women and girls delivers major benefits for society."
—Jimmy Carter, former United States president, and winner of the Nobel Peace Prize

Male or female, when it comes to gender equality, our country's solution is very simple: pay women and men equally for the same jobs, and treat everyone the same when it comes to benefits, parenting, and family issues. That's it. Take gender out of the equation and focus on the job performance and the character of the individual. I've been doing that successfully for many years in many different countries and there is no reason why this approach cannot be successful in every workplace in America.

Sadly, gender is not the only component of equality. Race, religion, age, accent, education, sexual orientation, height, weight, and a slew of other attributes can also cause some of us to be treated differently. As with gender, we are improving in most of these areas, but not fast enough to keep up with most of our successful global neighbors.

Here are a few of our former leaders' quotes when it comes to general equality. I find it interesting that these thoughts are just as relevant today as when they were spoken many years ago.

". . . a more equal liberty than has prevailed in other parts of the earth must be established in America."
—John Adams, in a letter to Patrick Henry, 1776

"Equal laws protecting equal rights; the best guarantee of loyalty and love of country."
—President James Madison, in a letter to Dr. Jacob de la Motta, 1820

"Equality, rightly understood as our founding fathers understood it, leads to liberty and to the emancipation of creative differences; wrongly understood, as it has been so tragically in our time, it leads first to conformity and then to despotism."
—Arizona Senator Barry Goldwater

Let's remember these thoughts and respect each other for our individual strengths. If we are to unite as a country, we have to include both men and women, young and old; black, white, yellow, and red, and all the many colors in between. We also have to find true equality in the areas of age, religion, sexual orientation and everything else that makes us "different" from each other. We all live here in the United States. That is our one common denominator, and if we are to become as great as we can be, we must forget our differences and pull together for the greater good of our country.

Maybe a new way of phrasing our greatness should be a small tweak to our original declaration: "We hold these truths to be self-evident, that all *people* are created equal."

AMERICA'S SIMPLE SOLUTIONS

Let's finally pay women and men equally for the same jobs. Take gender out of the equation and focus on the job performance and the character of the individual.

We must treat everyone the same when it comes to benefits, parenting, and family issues. There is nothing difficult about this. Let's just do it.

14

Business and Commerce

The rise and fall of a nation rests with every one of its citizens.
—Chinese Proverb, ancient wisdom for the twenty-first century

IF YOU DON'T BRING ANYTHING ELSE AWAY from your time reading this book I hope that, in addition to the importance of education, you understand that individual freedom produces wealth, advancement, and economic growth. And, that growth, great education, and personal betterment are the results of a system that encourages individual freedom. This typically happens in a capitalist, free market economy, one with the least amount of bureaucratic regulation.

Every person has hopes and dreams, and everyone should have the ability to realize those hopes and dreams in a manner that observes The Golden Rule. These dreams become reality in an environment of freedom, which (and this is no accident), is a place where wealth and innovation are high—due to the presence of freedom.

But, when I travel throughout the western world, including in America, I see an increase in cumbersome regulations, high taxes designed to create "wealth equality," and a central body of "political elite" who seem to feel they are the enlightened few who should determine what their fellow countrymen "must do." I see this, too, in countries where there is low or no growth. What is amazing is that the relationship between these unwise policies and the low or no growth is not acknowledged, or even recognized.

It is interesting that in Asia, these cumbersome and restrictive policies are *exactly* the policies that the rising Asian nations are abandoning. These ideas have already been tried there, and have been proven to be not effective. I see in my travels that a fast growing China and the developing Asian tigers are slowly adapting their capitalist system with more deregulation, and with the free market's idea of robust competition. These were the policies that made the west so successful in the first place and made western countries the leading economic powers in the world.

One might imagine a graph where there are two arrows: one pointing upward to represent the ascent and economic growth of Asia, and one pointing downward to represent the decline and low single digit growth of the US and the western world—including Japan. One area is adapting more freedom and capitalism, and is ascending in an increase toward a free market economy. The other sees more government control, socialistic policies of wealth leveling and "humanitarian" policies, and are experiencing stagnation. These countries are creating the very wealth inequality they are attempting to curtail.

I have numerous friends around the globe, which comes with the territory, given as much travel as I do. One of my friends of maybe twenty years is from Auckland, New Zealand. He visited me recently and shared his frustration with the policies of the US government with regard to foreigners who work temporarily in the US.

You see, my friend Manu Taylor is in the music business and represents a new young Kiwi band, all of whom are about eighteen years old. Manu has them on tour, playing in small venues in New York, and in places like Echo Park in Los Angeles where there are maybe eight hundred people in the audience. The band has certainly not reached star status yet, to say the least, but has a decent following. In business jargon, this music venture would be a "start up."

Manu explained to me that he had to pay roughly eleven thousand dollars to the US government for the right to perform in the US. This he had to pay at the US Consulate in New Zealand, prior to booking the trip and collecting the first dollar of revenue. He also had to fill out numerous forms, forms so cumbersome that he had to find an agent who specialized in these particular forms to make sure that all was done perfectly. This was all to get a visa to enter the US to perform, i.e. "work," for the two weeks of their tour. In the forms, Manu had to justify that his group was "internationally acclaimed" through press coverage for the last three years.

These kids are eighteen, so press coverage going back three years was a real challenge. Basically the visa money up front, the agent for the forms, and the government requirement of three years of press coverage already knocks out 98 percent of the applicants: kids with talent and dreams. This is why a young foreign group cannot perform in the US, unless a big company with a big budget brings them here. Then while these talented kids are here, there are multi-page tax forms, as well as forms for the act to get paid from the US employer that are equally cumbersome—and, the completion of these forms require an American to navigate it all. The result? Even more money paid out.

These burdensome regulations favor the wealthy and large companies, as they are the only ones that can pay to play. It also explains why they are the practically the only ones in the marketplace. In the music industry, Manu shared with me that the big players monopolize the market place and control the music. (An inordinate amount of regulation in any industry promotes monopoly as well.) This is just one more example where smothering government regulations knock out the little guy, crushes the hopes and dreams of young artists, thwarts competition, lowers the level of the product that makes it to the marketplace, and favors the big guys who monopolize it all. Who gets rich? Well, the wealthy because they are the only ones who can step up to this "ten-thousand-dollar limit poker table" and can afford to pay to play. This pattern is repeated over and over in every industry. The irony is that while our present day politicians are against wealth inequality, they are the ones creating it!

More and more, our marketplace is global. And, the mobile device in almost every young person's pocket exposes him or her to music from around the world. Music, like art, promotes cultural understanding, as well as entertainment, and the growth of the international music business is just that: growth. It is a real business that comes from entrepreneurial risk taking and contributes to employment in countries where it is created, and countries where it is heard.

The music business, and other global businesses, is not our government "stimulating" the economy by printing more money. With this new global music business model, the sales of music will create new jobs that are in harmony with our modern day times and technology. Certainly, however, one of the biggest obstacles to success with this business model are the many government regulations. Multiply this example in this one industry by a thousand, and then times a hundred more, and you get the gist of the problem. And we ask ourselves why there are no new jobs and why we have a declining middle class.

If you make something almost impossible to accomplish for the talented young dreamers of the world, then don't scratch your head and ask why there is no economic growth and no new jobs. This brings to mind another quote from Ronald Reagan, this one to the effect that the best form of social welfare is a job. Basically, if you make it impossible to create jobs, well, there won't be any. But, if your policies are such that you do everything to support and create jobs, then you will have a lot of them. This isn't complicated stuff.

> **If you make something almost impossible to accomplish for the talented young dreamers of the world, then don't scratch your head and ask why there is no economic growth and no new jobs.**

I have opened stores in numerous countries. I have imported goods from one economic zone to another. I have paid duties up the wazoo my entire professional life, and have had to overcome government regulations again and again to build successful international businesses. Obviously, any smart entrepreneur gravitates to an environment where the potential to succeed is high, and avoids an environment that breeds failure. This is common sense. Economic freedom brings about success, and in an environment of individual personal liberty, many young dreamers such as Steve Jobs, Mark Zuckerberg, and Bill Gates can succeed.

To make these important dreams happen, we must deregulate our western economies and support business by creating government services that support the businesses that employ 80 percent of our working population—small businesses. We need to lower taxes, celebrate success, and help our risk takers succeed.

Lee Kuan Lew is a great example of this. He is considered to be the founding father of Singapore, and his country has been described as transforming from a third world country to a first world country in a single generation, all under his leadership. Yes, it can be done. Strict government regulations not only stifle international business, but domestic business as well.

Here's an example. In November of 2014, my partners and I purchased a forty-two-thousand-foot warehouse in Commerce, California with the intention to house there our company distribution center, our retail warehouse, and the fulfillment center for our online business.
However, California is so over regulated, that every time a building changes hands, the new owner must then bring the building up to compliance with the standards of a newly built structure of today. Inflexible politicians in the US do not "grandfather" as is often done in Europe where sometimes businesses are housed in a Renaissance-era structure. To bring some buildings up to the standards of a newly-built structure is difficult and expensive, as the standards of bygone days were far different than they are today. Certain updates are not logical, and are not economically possible without almost demolishing the entire structure. Forget the aesthetic issues of how these huge changes might make the building look. Today we have so many modern building codes here in the US that address a tiny percent of buildings, that the imposition of the code is almost humorous.

To bring our new warehouse up to code, my company had to make more than six hundred thousand dollars in "improvements" to comply with all the government regulations. This was just so we could get an occupancy permit. We had to comply with ADA requirements, earthquake codes, asbestos abatement codes, plumbing codes, electrical codes, water codes, energy conservation codes, pallet rack construction codes, warehousing codes, insulation codes, and many others.

For example, 13 percent of the putty used in the 578 windows of our 1950-era building was asbestos. That was the composition of the putty that was used then, and at the time, it was thought to be the best material to use. That means that 87 percent of this material was not asbestos, so the danger of the presence of this 13 percent might rightfully be questioned.

Without going into the asbestos argument and its potential danger to humans, this 13 percent of asbestos mix had hardened into putty sixty-odd years ago, and had been painted over at least four times, sealing it from exposure to human beings. Plus, 90 percent of the windows were positioned in such a way, or at such a height, that people were unlikely to ever come within three feet of them.

But for the government, code is code, and regulations are regulations. It could be that we have a visitor one day in the warehouse who has a strong desire to sniff our windows. And if he or she sniffed hard enough, long enough, and with enough gusto, it just might be that this person could become sick from exposing him- or herself to this cement-like mix of painted over hardened putty that contains 13 percent asbestos. Thankfully, we have government regulations to safeguard people from this possibility.

Cost to replace windows: approximately twenty-five thousand dollars. Plus, we needed an inspection, and obviously, the inspector was busy inspecting all the other businesses that are ensnarled in these regulations, so he took time to get to us. As anyone who has done construction knows, subsequent work often depends on a final inspection of previous work, and this causes further delays.

The result to our business was that we had to pay for two warehouses for over six months, one to use, and one being prepared to use. This meant two staffs, two rents, two electrical bills, two of everything. This is a very unproductive use of capital, and shows just why US productivity is so abysmally low. We now actually rank far below our post-World War II productivity average. Not to mention that only a thriving business with a strong cash flow can bear this absurd burden. Most of our best, fresh, young, talented entrepreneurs are not in this game called business because they can't afford it—just more wealth inequality and impediments to success for our youthful entrepreneurs.

As a result of our economy's poor performance, the government has, many times, intervened into the marketplace to "jump start" our unproductive economy. How? They print more money to give the smothered economy some life. This actually creates more debt for our country, and this new debt is used to pay off the interest on the old debt. In the process of all this, businesses don't make money, so they don't pay much tax to the government, so the government doesn't make much money. The cycle goes on.

So why don't we have new jobs? Because this mindlessness, according to an April 29, 2015 *Wall Street Journal* article, has caused our economy to be stalled at 2 percent growth. This is the figure that has been announced by our government. If you don't believe their numbers, it is possible there is zero growth.

The good news is that there is a simple solution to all this: US businesses need a clear reduction in taxes and regulations to jump start the economy. It's as simple as that.

US businesses need a clear reduction in taxes and regulations to jump start the economy.

"Any system that penalizes success and accomplishment is wrong. Any system that discourages work, discourages productivity, discourages economic progress is wrong. If, on the other hand, you reduce tax rates and allow people to spend or save more of what they earn, they'll be more industrious; they'll have more incentive to work hard, and the money they earn will add fuel to the great economic machine that energizes our national progress. The result: more prosperity for all and more revenue for government."

—Ronald Reagan, 33rd governor of California (1967-1975), 40th president of the United States (1981-1989)

Remember, the longest economic expansion in our history came from Reagan and his policies in the early 1980s. Of note is this excerpt from a January 17, 1990 article in the New York Times: ". . . we do know from official economic statistics that the seven-year period from 1982 to 1989 was the greatest, consistent burst of economic activity ever seen in the U.S. In fact, it was the greatest economic expansion the world has ever seen—in any country, at any time." Remember, this was after a long decade of stagflation to cut taxes and to reduce regulations so business could once again thrive and flourish. I wonder what Reagan would have commented about my business's six-hundred-thousand-dollar expenditure in fulfilling all the government regulations in the building we purchased?

But Reagan, a Republican, wasn't the only one to advocate lowering taxes to stimulate business and increase revenues. This quote of democrat John F. Kennedy preceded his tax cut in the early 1960s:

"Our true choice is not between tax reduction on the one hand and avoidance of large federal deficits on the other; it is increasingly clear that no matter what party is in power, as long as our national security needs keep rising, an economy hampered by restrictive tax rates will never produce enough revenues to balance the budget—just as it will never produce enough jobs or enough profits. In short, the paradoxical truth is that the tax rates are too high today and tax revenues are too low and the soundest way to raise revenues in the long run is to cut rates now."

—John Fitzgerald Kennedy, 35th president of the United States (1961-1963)

I am in contact with corporate leaders across the globe, people who decide where they are going to place their corporate investments, and in which countries. These people make investment decisions with the sole purpose of getting the best return on their capital while minimizing their risk. Also, I have among my close friends some investment advisors and bankers who guide the funds of many international entrepreneurs and companies. And, among my acquaintances is a China-based legal firm that advises wealthy Chinese on where to globally place investments, and where to obtain foreign residency.

Among all these people, their general advice to their clients is: Don't invest in the United States. The taxes are penal, there are too many regulations, the government is non-supportive, the inheritance taxes are heavy, and the cost to file all the US government, state and local taxes is out of this world.

Among all these people, their general advice to their clients is: Don't invest in the United States.

I am specifically thinking of my friend, Daniel Salva. He is Spanish by passport, but has lived in France and worked at the highest echelons of publicly held and private European banks. These are banks that have sophisticated international corporate and high net worth individual clients. Without fail, it was the policy of these financial institutions to avoid investment in the United States at all costs.

As we've seen, only corporate giants are in a position to invest in America. Only they can subject themselves to our many regulations and taxes. Small international investors in the American dream sadly avoid the US, and are told to do so by far too many international investment advisors. We need to change this. We need to welcome all investors. If we do, we will see job growth again here in the US.

There is a video that the Hong Kong government put out a few years ago to promote Hong Kong as a place of business. We have already seen that Hong Kong has been a world leader in many areas: business growth, personal freedom, the financial success of its citizens, personal income, closeness of family, longevity, low unemployment, balanced budget, healthy welfare system, good health care, and so many other areas. It is also important to note that Hong Kong's primary interest is in commerce, and not in slaying foreign dragons. It might be that America could look at some aspects of Hong Kong's success, and emulate what is good. We can always learn from another's success.

It might be that America could look at some aspects of Hong Kong's success, and emulate what is good.

If you can, google the video. After you have seen the video, imagine a similar video put out by the US government, and with America being substituted for Hong Kong. I am envisioning a video that touts America as being business friendly, and as having an educated, willing, and skilled work force. This would be an America that has a low flat tax, respect for the rule of law, stability, a good geographical location for logistics (which America already does in the new global world), and is not involved in foreign conquest, but rather, is focused on commerce.

If all that were true, do you know what would happen? Investment would pour into America like never before. If America became openly business friendly, and we revived the American dream, which still exists in the minds of most of the entire world, within a short period of time there would be a job surplus here in the US. Workers could pick and choose their jobs, and real growth would be created—not paper printing growth, but the real stuff. Wages would rise, corporations would take their cash and reinvest it, the trillions of dollars that US corporations now keep overseas would return to our shores, and we could invest it in the education of the next generations. We could also rebuild our tired, worn-out infrastructure, and experience a boom bigger than that of the Industrial Revolution.

The dreams of each American citizen, with hard work, could then come true. All it will take is reducing the corporate tax on American businesses.

AMERICA'S SIMPLE SOLUTIONS

Too many regulations in any industry promotes monopoly. We must simplify these regulations if we are to keep free market enterprise alive and well, and if we are going to encourage the entrepreneurial spirit.

Our policies must be such that we do everything to support and create jobs. Then we will have a lot of them.

After we deregulate our economy we can support business by creating government services that support small businesses.

If we lower taxes, more small businesses will succeed. Even big business needs a clear reduction in taxes and regulations to jump-start the economy, so let's get on the phone to our lawmakers.

To survive, America must be business friendly and lower taxes will get us there.

We must also have an educated, willing, and skilled work force. Let's stop chasing foreign monsters that have not threatened us and use those dollars to educate our citizens and focus on commerce.

15

Technology

*Never before in history has innovation offered promise
of so much to so many in so short a time.*
—Bill Gates, founder, Microsoft

A FEW WEEKS AGO A CLOSE FRIEND of mine, a man I'll call Andre, came
over for dinner to watch the USC/Arizona State football game. As an active alumnus of USC and its graduate school, the Thunderbird Graduate
School of International Management in Glendale, Arizona (which was recently absorbed by Arizona State University), the game was of personal
interest to me. Andre also brought his twelve-year-old daughter, Siena,
along for the evening.

Siena was very polite, but was remarkably uninterested in the plight
of the two football teams on TV. She was far more interested in her cellular
device and in her constant communications with her friends. This occupied
all of her time and her full concentration for the first three quarters of

the game—until everyone sat down to dinner with the game on TV in the background.

To try to engage Siena and get her talking with the adults, I asked, "Facebook?" Her spontaneous reply was, "I'm not on Facebook, that's for old people. My friends and I only use Tumblr. It's so much better."

I then realized that Mark Zuckerberg, at thirty, was old news. For Siena's generation, he was way past his trendy prime, and Facebook just might be on the same trajectory as MySpace. Things move so fast in the world of technology, and Siena was certainly doing her part to keep up. In a recent lecture to the Iovine and Young Academy at USC I suggested to the group that fully half of them in fifteen years' time would be working in industries that not only don't exist today, these industries are not yet even imagined.

From phones, to television, to the many new features in our cars, technology dominates our world and will do so even more in the foreseeable future. Actually, I am writing this chapter on my Apple notepad on a 787 airplane, flying my way from Tokyo to Bangkok, thirty-five thousand feet in the air. Over the next two days I will have a number of meetings with my partners in Thailand and Southeast Asia.

The day before yesterday, however, instead of a plane I took the Japanese bullet train, the 250 mph Shinkansen, from Tokyo to Osaka. I had meetings in the morning in Osaka, then reboarded the bullet train and after a short but very fast ride I had a meeting in Kyoto. After all that, I still had time to visit one of the most beautiful and moving eleventh century Japanese shrines, the Sanjusangendo Temple. This Buddhist masterpiece features roughly one thousand exquisitely carved and gold gilded soldiers within the temple.

After my visit to the temple. I took the Shinkansen back to Tokyo and spent my time speaking on my iPhone to my office in Los Angeles, with my team in Bangkok, and taking pictures out the window. (Thank you again, Steve Jobs, for such a wonderful technological device as the iPhone.) Then I edited the pictures I had just taken and created collages of them before I Instagrammed them world wide. Even though it was an "old fashioned" activity, I also had a few minutes to make comments to my friends on Facebook, learn what they were up to, look at pictures of their life events, and read what they were thinking about.

Yes, technology today is truly amazing, especially when you are my age and have lived the majority of your life without it. There is no way I could have completed all of that travel or been that productive during my travel even two decades ago.

In another example, a few days before all of this, I was in Shanghai working with our Japanese manufacturers who are based there. I also had meetings with my China partners about new store development for our American Rag stores in new Chinese cities. These meetings involved the potential of an additional Chinese partner, one whose company has already opened 1600 stores throughout China. This new proposed venture was to be financed by a Hong Kong fund, and owned and staffed by nationals from the United Kingdom, the United States, and Italy. Talk about our new global world, this is it!

Most of the people I do business with internationally are tri-lingual at the least, and rapidly learn new languages with the help of computerized programs such as Rosetta Stone. This is yet another way that technology is changing the way the world works.

Why am I telling you all this? If you had read this as recently as one hundred years ago when cars were first making their appearance (and had constant flat tires in Southern California due to the lack of roads) you might think you had just read an excerpt from a book of science fiction. Yet the planes I travel on are almost always full, and how I do business is now common and accepted in just about every country around the world. All of this is the result of one, single phenomenon that has made unbelievable advances in the last century: technology.

Today, technology is an essential tool of political freedom, indeed of personal freedom itself.

Technology is not just part of futurism, travel, communication, instant information, and convenience. It is not just a social tool that allows you to be in contact with your existing friends or meet new ones. Today, technology is an essential tool of political freedom, indeed of personal freedom itself.

I wonder what enlightened observations our Founding Fathers would have made about the technology that we have today? I think they would have seen it as a tool, something that could be used to deter the encroachment of personal liberty, as James Madison feared.

Technology is definitely being used to mobilize political action in ways our forefathers could have never imagined. The Arab Spring was a recent series of revolutionary demonstrations, protests, riots, and civil wars in the Arab world that began in 2010 in Tunisia, and spread throughout the countries of the Arab League. It sprang from numerous local rallies that were organized by mobile devices, so in this way technology is even being used to mobilize revolutions.

Mass communication through the use of mobile devices can happen either when there is a lot of freedom in an individual country, or when there is a lack of it. Here we have Amber alerts and weather warnings that come to most of us through our smartphones. And, Barack Obama was the first US presidential candidate to take the use of social media to stratospheric levels. Obama aside, one tweet by a celebrity is instantly received by millions of followers. That is some powerful stuff.

This kind of delivery of information is available to all, instantly, unless the government restricts it. This, sadly, is the case in many countries throughout the world, and perhaps most notoriously, the new super power we call China. In some countries in the world today, though, rapid and dramatic political change is coming about solely because of technology.

Brazil is one such country. The name Kim Kataguiri is a household name there, since he is one of several who founded the social movement group, Movimento Brasil Livre. This group is calling to impeach their allegedly corrupt president. Dilma Roussef, who happens to be the first female president of that country. The call for impeachment came about due to the enormous debt Roussef ran up for Brazil in a short period of time. Plus, there is a scandal of kickbacks surrounding Petrobras, a huge semi-public multi-national energy conglomerate headquartered in Brazil's Rio de Janeiro, is part of it as well.

Kim Kataguiri is a young activist who, with the help of several friends, organized this impeachment movement via his mobile devices. He has also made many low budget YouTube videos on his smartphone that highlight and promote his movement, videos that tug at heartstrings and pull at people's emotions.

Kim organized one protest that more than two hundred thousand people attended. Recently, more than a million people attended another of Kim's protests in Sao Paolo, Brazil, the country's largest city. This protest set the record for the most protesters at any event in Brazil since the 1980 protests that demanded democratic elections.

These recent protests were all organized through mobile technology. From Twitter to Tumblr to Instagram and even "old fashioned" Facebook, to smartphones, tablets, and other mobile devices, we live and work in a brand new world. To be effective, as Kim Kataguiri has been, we all have to keep up with at least some of it.

Kataguiri has been called a liberal and a radical for supporting such dangerous principles as "freedom and democracy," and for promoting such "radical" economic thinkers as Milton Friedman. Friedman was an American economist who received the 1976 Nobel Memorial Prize in economic sciences and was an advisor to both Ronald Reagan and British Prime Minister Margaret Thatcher. He passed on in 2006. I find it interesting that Kim's heroes also include such so-called "subversives" as Ronald Reagan and Margaret Thatcher.

Not too long ago young Kim Kataguiri became fed up with Brazil's soaring inflation, the debasing of the Brazilian currency, and the corruption of the politicians; as well as how those in power crush the dreams, hopes, and aspirations of his young generation. But Kim is not just complaining. He is doing something about these injustices by organizing widely-attended protests through the technology of his mobile device.

Kataguiri's success shows the potential impact that technology has on the political life of a country. Citizens nationwide can communicate with each other, and can demand the freedoms they deserve. Technology can also bring insights into the corrupt activities of politicians and cause them to be more accountable. Our next generation is growing up with a mobile device in their pockets at all times. They will have access to instant information and research, and are not going to be placid when it comes to their own rights and freedoms. How could our next generation just silently accept the mountain of debt our present political leaders are leaving them to cope with, and simply say nothing?

Kim Kataguiri is slightly ahead of his time and I encourage you to google his videos and to spend a few minutes watching them. They impacted me greatly. I know that his wide-spread message of impeachment in the face of corruption, and his passion for allowing young people to realize their dreams and hopes through technology is not going to be the only time this happens. Politicians beware! Change is coming.

In addition to the activities of politicians on national and worldwide stages, our new technology will also allow mundane things such as office communication, doctor visits, and inefficient medical systems that overcharge patients to become more visible as well. Oppressive regulations will be easier to identify, and indeed, almost every aspect of our lives will be impacted by the daily, sometimes hourly, advancement of technology. The biggest revolution since the Industrial Revolution is happening right now, so fasten your seat belts. It's going to be a wild ride.

We all need to be ready to embrace this rapid change, because change will be the standard and not the exception. Countries and individuals who are left behind on the technology front will not be able to compete for jobs. They will not be competitive in manufacturing, travel, staffing, sales, marketing, production, or any other area of business or commerce. This inability to keep up with the rest of the world means that the economy of a country that lags behind will also suffer. That's why it is imperative that we not only keep up, but that we lead the charge into new technological frontiers. But, we absolutely need the freedom to do so.

Countries and individuals who are left behind on the technology front will not be able to compete for jobs.

The solution for the average American to this rapid change is another simple one: education. Common sense demands that we all stay ahead of this tidal wave of technology. To achieve this, we must educate our kids using the best and newest technology that we can. This goes for adults as well. We must have computers for every student in every classroom, and each person needs a mobile device and educational access to the Internet. We must, of course, set limits and parameters for our children's use of the Internet and the technology that is already here, even though many parents do not make use of it.

According to a 120-page study done in 2014 by McKinsey & Company, an advisor and counselor to many of the world's largest businesses and institutions, 4.4 billion people across the globe have no access to the Internet—and fifty million of those people are here in the United States. In fact, according to the study, we are nineteenth when it comes to poor Internet access for our students and citizens. Nineteenth? This doesn't concern us?

How can we possibly compete on a worldwide stage, how can the United States of America possibly become a world leader when we are nineteenth in Internet access? Lack of access to the Internet is a huge marker of inequality, especially as roughly half of low-income families nationwide do not have and cannot afford Internet service.

"Addressing the widening gap between the rich and poor in the United States could help improve affordability of Internet access for those at the bottom of the pyramid," the study states. This means that until we find a way to fund some level of free Internet access for everyone, some measure of our population will always be left behind. Once again, funds become available from productive growth and job creation, and our own government is the biggest impediment to these two important factors. The US must make a conscious decision to become business friendly and remove regulations that stifle business and young entrepreneurs. Only then will a miracle happen, and will funds become available.

The US must make a conscious decision to become business friendly and remove regulations that stifle business and young entrepreneurs.

If you are behind the wave of technology as an adult, you must make it a priority to educate yourself and catch up. Do it now. Take an adult education class in computers, the Internet, web design, or social media. You could also ask your kids or grandkids to help you. When you become fully aware of this revolution of technology, you will love it.

Another simple solution is that we must go into the voting booths and elect officials who embrace technological change. Politicians who do not support technology in our schools or some kind of free Internet access that is available to everyone also holds every single other part of our country back, including in the areas of jobs, employment, economy, education, and every other area we need to excel in if we are to be great. Plus, pretty soon we'll all vote with our mobile devices, and it will be effortless to obtain all the information we need to have about candidates in our local, state, and national elections.

Here's the bottom line. If all Americans took it upon themselves to educate themselves in the newest technology, our productivity would flourish. And, in the absence of excessive regulations and punishing taxes from our government, our national growth will restart in a hurry. It is as simple as that.

AMERICA'S SIMPLE SOLUTIONS

Today's technology revolution is as great as the great industrial revolution of the past, if we do not board the train now, it will have left the station. This is just one more reason why we absolutely have to educate our kids.

Technology is driven by education. It is one of our most important simple solutions, but can only be achieved with great teachers, who must be paid competitive salaries.

To be foster technical minds, we must have computers for every student in every classroom, and each person needs a mobile device and educational access to the Internet.

16

Crime and Gun Control

A well regulated Militia, being necessary to the security of a free State,
the right of the people to keep and bear Arms, shall not be infringed.
—the Second Amendment to the Constitution of the
United States of America

I WAS BORN IN LOS ANGELES IN 1945. While California actually became a
state almost one hundred years before my arrival on earth, its largest city,
Los Angeles, didn't really become an international metropolis until some
time in the 1980s.

When I was growing up there was still a small town feeling of a clus-
ter of communities that had an old, American main street feel. There was
Azusa, Monrovia, Palos Verdes, Palm Springs, Brentwood, Van Nuys, Santa
Ana, Newport Beach, and many others. Los Angeles was not a big city
then, and was more a grouping of small towns. The population of the city
of Los Angeles at that time was nearly three million, but spread out over

a wide area. You can still find this small town, main street feeling today in some communities outside of Los Angeles, such as Ojai and Moorpark.

When I was growing up my family lived in a little East Hollywood area called Los Feliz, and the local A&P Market was on Vermont Avenue. My father's medical office was also on Vermont, above the Bank of America, and whenever I went to the grocery store with my mom, or the drug store, or to get a haircut at the local barber, I met many familiar faces, some from church. "Good morning, or "good afternoon" was an obligatory greeting, depending on the time of day.

I remember the first "round tube" TV dad brought home, and in those times in our home, the "rooten-tooten" cowboy films of the Old West played over and over. This was the only place my family and I ever saw guns— on TV. My siblings and I played cowboys and Indians, and I had little leather chaps and Indian feathers. We weren't very "PC" back then.

My favorite program on Sunday was the one with Hopalong Cassidy and his trusty sidekick, Cochise the Indian. I also had a choice of Tex Ritter, singing cowboy Gene Autry, Tex Williams, or any of the other 1940s cowboy movie stars whom I idolized. John Wayne came a little later, but that ex-USC football star was already an up and coming cowboy tough guy in the early days of television.

My brothers, friends, and I all had toy guns. But when I asked my mom and dad if I could get a real BB gun, their stern looks immediately answered my question. I was told that "guns were dangerous, we don't have guns in this household, and that if I had a good education, I wouldn't ever need a gun." I wasn't completely convinced, since little Chuck Laurence down the street had a BB gun. Sometimes I snuck off to play with Chuck, and we'd shoot BBs in the back yard.

The summer I was six, my brother and I went to a Catholic camp for boys for two weeks. The camp was in the Lake Arrowhead area, and some of the camp counselors let me shoot a BB gun. I was in heaven, especially when I learned that I had won the top award for six year olds for shooting. With my newfound skill, I shot and killed a few small animals, such as lizards and frogs. I never forgot those first shooting experiences because it was something that was not allowed at home under any circumstances.

Despite my BB experience, I still thought that real guns were only on TV. The idea of a teenager shooting a gun at a high school was unthinkable.

When I was seventeen I got a job moving furniture with Bekins Van Lines. California was booming, as there was a mass migration to our sunny state. My work at Bekins kept me very busy and I made more money than any of my friends, although I worked some pretty long hours. I also became strong as an ox through the constant lifting.

In 1964, during the hot summer months, race riots erupted in south central Los Angeles, in an area called Watts. One day at work I was given an unloading job right in the middle of Watts, even though the National Guard was still on the streets there. I was a driver's assistant, and I remember my driver balking at the assignment because of the possible danger. Occasional incidents of looting were still going on. Plus, there was an "overly reactive police force" (police brutality) that was prevalent at that time.

We arrived at the warehouse where we were to unload, and the National Guard immediately surrounded our truck so that we would not be attacked and looted during the unloading. They were heavily armed and the images from that day have stayed in my mind.

After I finished graduate school, I moved to Europe and lived there until 1984 when I returned to the US. During my time in Europe very few people had guns because the countries there rarely allowed them. Hunters had to go through a stringent screening process, and in most of the European countries, had to have a license to own a gun. Even the "bobbies," the police in England, didn't carry guns.

In Holland I remember hearing a gun shot just once during the many years I lived in Amsterdam, although knives, knifing, and robbery with a knife unfortunately happened fairly regularly. Once, my Rotterdam store was robbed at knifepoint. My staff was tied up and the robbers made off with the day's receipts. Robbers still robbed, even without guns, but killings with a knife were rare.

Winston Churchill once said something to the effect that if you're not liberal and a socialist at age twenty-one you have no heart, but if you are still a liberal and a socialist at thirty-one you have no brain. Whether you subscribe to Churchill's statement or not, I was very social in my twenties. I thought the US was nuts to still prescribe to the Second Amendment, to allow people to have guns, and I thought the amendment was archaic and should be annulled.

In 1984, however, I moved back to California and opened my present retail company, American Rag Cie, and in 1985, we leased a large building on La Brea Ave. I worked hard, and built my business from scratch. I poured my heart and soul into my business and made it a success. It was my life, my family, my hobby, my love, and my work. I built it from zero and felt a huge pride of ownership—as I still do today.

In 1992 my oldest son, Julian, was attending USC. One Wednesday night at the end of April he called me around ten PM to say he was driving down the Harbor Freeway toward Long Beach and saw hundreds of fires. "There are fires around campus," he said, "but through South Central it looks like the entire city is on fire."

We'd later learn that the fires were the beginning of riots that started after a jury acquitted four Los Angeles police officers of using excessive force in the videotaped arrest and beating of a man named Rodney King. Thousands of people in Los Angeles rioted for more than six days following the verdict. Widespread looting, assault, arson, and killings occurred during the riots, and the estimated property damage was more than one billion dollars. The rioting ended after members of the California Army National Guard, the 7th Infantry Division, and the 1st Marine Division were called in when local police realized they could not handle the situation. In total, fifty-three people were killed, over two thousand people were injured, and more than eleven thousand were arrested.

All of that we learned later. In this moment, however, I wasn't sure what was going on. I asked my son if he was safe, and after an affirmative answer I quickly hung up and called my partner, Rudolphe Faulcon, who lived down the street from me. I remembered the Watts Riots, what had happened twenty years before, and took action.

When I awakened Rudolphe, I said, "I need you to get your guns, every gun you can find." Rudolphe is French and many in the Los Angeles French community were gun lovers who shot recreationally on weekends. I added that I would pick him up in five minutes and asked him to bring his old pick up truck. I wanted to park the truck on the sidewalk in front of the store and spend the night there. Rudolphe thought I had lost my mind. "Aren't you over reacting?" he asked. "No. Trust me," I said, "I'll be there in five."

We arrived at the La Brea store, put the truck on the sidewalk in front of the door, and horizontally placed our rifles behind the seat. We kept two loaded rifles on our laps and spent the night there in front of the store. Initially, I was uncomfortable with the guns. But as the night progressed, a number of buildings near our block were set ablaze, and we watched cars race down La Brea with a total disregard for traffic lights and the speed limit. A few cars slowed down as they passed us, but after viewing what appeared to be gun ready vigilantes, they kept going.

The next day the situation didn't get any better. In fact, it got worse, dramatically worse. As I had a payroll coming up on Monday, I tried to keep the store open. When the staff arrived we left the truck on the sidewalk with the guns visible inside, but moved it so it wasn't blocking the door. Then I asked Rudolphe to call everyone he knew who had a gun to see if we could get some help. We rounded up a couple of French nationals and a Dutch male model, and we all stayed inside the store for the duration of the riots, fully armed. You see, insurance doesn't cover "civil disorder or acts of war" and what was going on was certainly a civil disorder. It was my company, my home, my children and me—against them. That's it.

As tensions rose, rioters began shooting at the firemen who were trying to put out the fires, so many of the firemen abandoned their jobs and fled. Next were the police, many of whom who also fled their posts and left Los Angeles to total anarchy and chaos. At the height of the riots on Thursday afternoon the sky was black, because there were as many as eight thousand buildings on fire throughout the city. It was out and out war.

Around noon on Thursday there was a rumor of a shooting inside the Beverly Center, which was not far away. My staff got word of this, panicked, and left the store, so I called our security company and asked for any available guards who could carry a gun. I then called my childhood friend, Peter Daniels of HG Daniels Artist Supplies, and asked Pete if he had any large pieces of Styrofoam that I could use to board up our windows against the Molotov cocktails and pipe bombs. Pete sent over a stack of Styrofoam boards, and Rudolphe and I boarded up all the windows.

Just then "Jaime," showed up from our security firm. He was a take charge security guard from El Salvador who shared that he had been through this sort of looting, rioting, and burning in his own country. He also had three more guards scheduled to arrive later in the day.

Inside our boarded up store we had the radio tuned to a station that was reporting all the news and chaos. The station constantly asked the public to not go out on the streets because there was no police or fire department, and things were totally out of control.

At one point a car stopped in front of the store, and a passenger got out and taunted us as we huddled inside. Jaime stepped forward, put his hand on his gun and froze with his chest out, giving a glacial stare to the would be looter and arsonist. It was after this that we decided we were sitting ducks inside the boarded up store, so Jaime ordered everyone onto the roof "pronto. We're moving," he barked at us.

I had a handgun in my belt directly above my zipper and carried a rifle. This was my outfit for the next four or five days: a gun in my belt and a rifle in my hands. Everyone else was armed, as well. As we climbed the ladder to the roof, the three other guards arrived.

Jaime ordered each of us to take a position at the front of the store, from corner to corner on the roof, and to hold our rifles so they were visible to everyone below. It was wild, and I went from never having had a real gun in my hands, to intimately knowing that, without guns, my business would be burned to the ground.

No one stopped in front of the store for very long once they saw the American Rag militia on the roof. One of the late arriving guards was an overweight Salvadorian. I wondered if he was of any value, other than just a physical presence of someone holding a gun, as he moved very slowly. I remember that "Miguel" spoke slowly, too. As it turned out, slow

Miguel shot at the feet of would be looters and arsonists three times. I was glad that the noise of the bullets hitting the sidewalk in front of them discouraged any further interest in my building, and in us.

I admit that I was scared to death. My mouth was so dry that I constantly had to drink water, and then I couldn't swallow. I contemplated my own death as the fires raged on and filled the sky with smoke. Later that day I got Jaime to engage another armed security guard to stand post at the beginning of the street that I lived on in the Hollywood Hills. I didn't want my house to be set ablaze and I worried about the well-being and safety of my wife and child.

One of our armed "Frenchies" was an employee of American Rag, a denim expert named Christophe Loiron. He came from Aix en Provence near Marseille in the southern part of France. Months earlier he had set up a visit with one of his childhood friends from Aix and it just so happened that his friend arrived in the middle of all the anarchy. He arrived Thursday afternoon in a taxi in front of the store and looked up to see us all armed on the roof. Christophe yelled to him in French to *fait le tour*, go around the back, and climb up the ladder to the roof with his bags.

So, this eighteen-year old Frenchman, who was visiting the US for the first time, climbed the ladder around the back and got up on the roof. Jaime, ever the Latino alpha male, ordered our fresh replacement to take a position in the far corner of the roof, threw him a Winchester, and said to make himself visible with his rifle to those below. I remember that the young Frenchman, eyes big, said in French something to the effect of, "this is so cool! Is it always like this here in Los Angeles?"

The riots went on for three or four more days. We were there on the roof 24/7 until finally, on Sunday afternoon George H. W. Bush got the National Guard and some other military units into the streets and some semblance of order was restored. As an interesting aside, the National Guard had actually arrived on Saturday, but someone failed to include ammunition for their rifles, so the rioting continued for another day.

My time during the Rodney King riots came down to self-defense and the experience changed my perspective on guns. After, I purchased a few rifles (a Remington and a Winchester), a Beretta handgun, and took courses on how to use them safely. Although I rarely think about my guns today, I still have them and I keep them under lock and key.

In the days that followed the riots, we had letters from almost everyone on our block, thanking us for protecting their life, their property, their families, and their businesses. Two weeks later, as I drove down La Brea, I saw burned buildings on every block of La Brea Ave, except ours. It was as pristine as if nothing has happened. Our second amendment kept me, and many others, safe.

In addition to the issue of self-defense, the United States is a big country, and there are many rural areas that are teeming with wild animals. We live next to Griffith Park in the Los Feliz district of Los Angeles. In the hills behind our home lives P22, a puma who has crossed freeways to feast on the deer population in the park. There are also packs of coyotes, and I mean packs. The other night there were more than a dozen wild dogs howling in the night, right next to our house where my children play. They have already attacked and eaten several pets on our street, including one of our own, and we are constantly vigilant to never leave our young twins alone outside.

Then, because humans have killed off many of their natural predators, the deer and wild game population often explodes. I, personally, could never kill a deer unless it was for survival, but if someone wants to hunt deer or other game, as long as it is done safely following The Golden Rule, hunting is part of our individual freedom as Americans.

Environmentalists often say "they were here first." True, but why would you want packs of wild, blood-thirsty dogs running around where there are small children? There was a serious coyote attack in nearby Burbank a couple of years ago and a two-year-old girl was badly injured. After a coyote attacked our dog, and attacked a woman in front of our house who was walking her dog, I spoke with the local park ranger. He informed me they have specific instructions not to harm the coyotes.

Let's talk solutions. There are millions of coyotes in the United States, and the Griffith Park pack and other packs could be relocated to a wildlife area where they would integrate into the cycle of nature there, without endangering children.

We can also create feeding stations far away from populated areas and lace the feed with contraceptives. The wild animal population would then eventually be kept under control. The cost of either of these ideas would be less than the cost of the many man hours that go into tracking, capturing, removing, and sometimes euthanizing dangerous animals who stray too close to places where people live. Plus, we'd all be safer.

However, if it ever came to a choice between the safety of my twins or saving the lives of some wild dogs, it would not take me a millisecond to make that choice. I am glad that I have the guns to handle that undertaking, and will gladly do so if the need arises.

All that being said, there is an obvious lack of intelligent control of firearms in America today. The National Rifle Association won't agree with me, but we must have required safety training for every gun owner. We also need to have a safety firearms test for gun owners, just as we have driving tests for drivers. Both cars and guns are potentially lethal. There's no difference. No one objects to a driving test as an infringement of individual freedom.

We must have required safety training for every gun owner.

When it comes so driving under the influence of alcohol, that is illegal and the same should apply to someone with a gun in their hand. Felons, the mentally ill, minors, and other carefully considered categories of people should also not be allowed to have guns. Period.

According to bradycampaign.org, the firearm homicide rate is *twenty* times higher in the US than the *combined* rates of twenty-two countries that are our peers in wealth and population. And, American children die by guns *eleven* times as often as children in other high-income countries.

This is why we need background checks—for everyone, every time they purchase a new gun. Our current background check system only applies to about 60 percent of gun sales. This leaves 40 percent (online sales, purchases at gun shows, etcetera) without any background check at all. Flea market vendors who sell used firearms to anyone who shows up? That doesn't make sense. In looking at the many school, theater, and other mass shootings in public places in America, virtually every one of those shooters would not have passed a background check. Yes, some might have found guns anyway, but others would not have. Just think of the lives that could have been saved.

We need background checks—for everyone, every time they purchase a new gun.

Gun ownership doesn't have to be an all or nothing proposition. I get what founding father James Madison said, that the government trusts the people to "bear arms." This was originally added as an amendment to prevent the potential of a dictatorial government. We must examine where we are with this concept today and consider several things. Is it a right (or a personal freedom) to go into a school or a movie theater and kill people? We must also consider if our government has encroached upon our personal freedom when it comes to gun control. And if so, to what point? I get the gun lovers' concern about where to draw the line on government encroachment of our personal freedom. The government has already usurped too much of our personal freedom, but we must come together to draw the line.

I get what founding father James Madison said, that the government trusts the people to "bear arms." This was originally added as an amendment to prevent the potential of a dictatorial government.

This is a difficult issue, for sure. Using technology that can be found in "smart guns," guns that won't fire unless held by an accredited, safety-instructed gun owner is another solution. And certainly, our dysfunctional court system should not be so "understanding" toward those who violate our gun safety standards.

When it comes to gun control, we must put aside our differences and instead come together to develop reasonable standards for gun ownership. So let's get leaders and experts from all sides of the issue together to set these standards. There has to be middle ground here and now is the time to find it. Then we must get courts to enforce the new gun laws. Only then will we have any sense of safety in our country, while still having the right to protect ourselves.

AMERICA'S SIMPLE SOLUTIONS

Let's not confuse "the right to organize a militia" with the right to shoot a dozen kids in a schoolyard with a semi-automatic weapon.

Gun control does not have to be an either/or situation when it comes to gun ownership. All sides need to come off their high horse, sit down together, and work this out. Yes, most of us have the right to bear arms, but certain segments of the population, such as those who have a severe mental illness, felons, and other such people should not own a weapon.

Rather than shoot them, packs of wild animals that stray too closely to populated areas could be relocated to wildlife areas to integrate into the cycle of nature there.

Feeding stations far away from populated areas can be laced with contraceptives to keep wild animal populations under control.

Our dysfunctional court system should not be so "understanding" toward those who violate our gun safety standards. We need to set harsher punishments and stick by them.

17

Oil and the Middle East

America does not go abroad in search of monsters to destroy.
—John Quincy Adams, Sixth President of the United States
(1825-1829), son of John Adams, Second President of the
United States (1794-1801)

No nation could preserve its freedom in the midst of continual warfare.
—James Madison, Fourth President of the United States
(1809-1817), Master Builder of the Constitution

*Peace, commerce, and honest friendship with all nations;
entangling alliances with none.*
—Thomas Jefferson, author, Declaration of Independence,
Third President of the United States (1801-1809)

DURING MY ENTIRE LIFETIME, THERE HAS BEEN a religious war raging in
the Middle East. At a recent dinner party with my fellow board members

at USC, we exchanged pleasantries before dinner and I shared this observation. Someone in the group corrected me and said, "Mark, that situation goes back more than five hundred years before you arrived." Point taken.

I have used the analogy of a "bad neighborhood" before, and this certainly includes the Middle East. In case there was any doubt, the 2015 terrorist events on European and North African soil, along with constant threats directed at cities around the world, confirmed this bad neighborhood idea, especially as the majority of the terrorists originated from a Middle Eastern country.

To be clear, the Middle East is an overly broad name for a large and extremely complex group of nations that stretches from the North African Maghreb to Iran. Some might argue that the term should also include Muslim Pakistan and Afghanistan. In either case, one might call the combination of these countries the Muslim nations.

Most of us know there are two major Muslim blocks, the Sunnis and the Shiites. There are also a few other minor branches of this religion in eastern North Africa. Then there are the Kurds, and the blue people—the Berbers of the Atlas Mountains of Morocco. Almost all of them have had some sort of conflict with another group in the region. This has been the case for centuries, and continues today.

The geography across the Middle East comes into play in this fighting, especially as the topography and weather is diverse. You can ski in Morocco and Lebanon, and there are warm weather sports and beach resorts almost everywhere, but the wide variety of terrain allows many places for terrorists to congregate, train, and hide. There also has been much conflict over access to the sea and shipping routes.

Because the history of the area is ancient and complex, and the traditions and ways of survival run many centuries deep, we just don't need to get involved. Period. In fact, let's just stay home and take care of our own problems.

The situation is especially complex because when dealing with trouble in the Middle East, we are not always dealing with a specific country. Libya, for example, is made up of many loyal familial tribes that take precedence over a sense of nation. Then there is the fact that those in Egypt and Saudi

Arabia both feel that they are the center of Arab culture. There are also many national enemies within these nations that, by far, predate western colonization and the influence of the west. Just who are we to think we can change centuries of hurts, war, and hatred?

There is also the idea in the Middle East, in many countries there anyway, that women are seen as a lower level of human than a man is. In some countries there, a woman's rights are severely restricted. Plus, stoning, public torture, and the severing of limbs for the crime of theft still occur. Languages, dialects, and local accents run in the hundreds, although Arabic is the main language outside of Iran and the Kurdish states. All of this combines to mean that the Arab world generally does not prescribe to western values, but has their own value system that includes long-practiced customs, traditions, and religion.

Just who are we to think we can change centuries of hurts, war, and hatred?

According to the Legatum Prosperity Index, the general level of education in that part of the world is low. A call to prayer is heard five times a day, blasted on loud speakers in almost every country. Alcoholic beverages are typically not served, except in places that cater to tourists.

During a recent trip to Dubai, certainly one of the most western and advanced modern cities in the Arab world, I noted a few things of interest. My wife and I had a five-bedroom suite in one of the Marriott branded hotels, with two balconies that overlooked a yacht harbor. The large kitchen was state-of-the-art and we could have cooked for thirty guests, as it was fully stocked with all sorts of dishes, and pots and pans. The décor was nice, but not over the top, and it was clear that the suite was set up for a large family that had domestic help. Price for the entire suite: $175 a night in overbuilt Dubai.

In contrast, that evening we went out to dinner to a fine restaurant with a western menu, and the bill for six guests was seventeen hundred dollars! That's almost three hundred dollars a person. The chic local Arab women at the restaurant either wore chadors, the traditional head-to-toe garment of Muslim and Hindu women, or a burka, which also covers the face. I have to say that I never saw such an assortment of expensive designer purses and shoes. One might think that thousand dollar and above glitzy footwear from Manolo Blahnik were required dress.

The next day we visited a large Dubai mall, the one where the immense multi million-gallon shark tank exploded in 2010 and flooded the mall with sharks and all sorts of other species of sea fish. Our visit happened a few years after that and I noted, as I had seen in the restaurant, the inventory in the Vuitton, Gucci, Tom Ford, and other luxury shops was 80 percent purses and shoes. It's a different world for women who have to wear a burka.

When we returned to the hotel in a taxi, as we approached the front door of the hotel, an Arab gentleman in a black suit approached me without glancing at my wife. "Sir," he said, "who is this woman?" Puzzled, I replied, "My wife." Then he said, "Please come right in." The next night after going out to eat, we returned to the hotel, and the same dude in the black suit approached me again. "Sir, who is this woman?" I replied with a slight degree of annoyance, "My wife," to which he replied once again, "Please come right in." Once in the hotel, I turned to Amanda and wondered who the guy was. But then I forgot about him, because in the Middle East there are always elements of the unusual and exotic.

However, on our third night at the hotel, the same thing occurred. Totally annoyed, I replied, "No change. We haven't gotten a divorce today. She's still my wife." He again replied, unfazed, "Sir, please step right in."

This time I went to the reception desk and pointed to the man at the front door. "Who is that guy who approaches us every time we return to the hotel at night?" I asked.

"He is the morality police," the man at the desk replied.

"Do you mean the sex police?" I asked. "Could you please inform him that Mrs. Werts and I are happily married and do not plan to divorce, and that we certainly will stay married during the remainder of our stay in Dubai, so he doesn't have to ask us every night?"

It's obvious that there is a different culture in place in the Middle East, one that is very different from Iowa, Oregon, Florida, or Minnesota.

A city like Boston or San Francisco would never exist in the Middle East. It absolutely is not our world.

The Middle East is also much different than Europe. I once read an article in a Dutch paper about a Moroccan family that was cooking a lamb on their marble living room floor, much to the chagrin of the other co-tenants in the Dutch apartment complex. Middle Easterners also don't abandon their culture easily when they move to the west, because their culture is as beautiful and sacred to them as their religion is.

I understand that. I understand being ingrained into a culture, and loving the traditions your family has practiced for generations. I also love many things about the Middle East. If you saw my home, you'd see that I have a personal love affair with the exoticism and the culture of the Arab world. I have sold Moroccan and Arabic ceramics for years, and have sold Moroccan tile for more than twenty years. I find these to be some of the most beautiful tiles in existence.

I also love the food, the music there is sublime, and I cannot think of a more beautiful place on earth than Marrakesh. Indeed, I had an office for three years in Casablanca, and have returned to that area of the world on many occasions. The only reason I didn't learn to speak Arabic is that all the factory owners I dealt with in Morocco spoke fluent French, and when I made an effort in Arabic, they consistently admonished me to "stop that nonsense," so I never had a chance with the language.

To our Founding Father John Quincy Adams, the Middle East would certainly fall under the word "abroad." That is for sure. And his admonition was that we should not go abroad "seeking monsters to destroy." The Middle East is clearly not our world. It is neither good nor bad, just very different, and we certainly have no business judging their value system, or trying to impose our values on them—as long as they do not bother us. As Thomas Jefferson said, "Peace, commerce, and honest friendship with all nations, entangling alliance with none."

As Thomas Jefferson said, "Peace, commerce, and honest friendship with all nations, entangling alliance with none."

Unfortunately, we didn't listen. Not when it came to the religions of the Middle East, and not when it came to their culture. Certainly we didn't listen when it came to their oil. So many of our politicians argue that it is in our economic interest to be in the Middle East because we need the oil that is produced there. Oil is the very basis of our developed world and way of life and they have so much of it.

I get their point. Certainly a field plowed by a single farmer with an ox is vastly less productive that a field plowed by a motorized vehicle that is able to plow many acres in a single day. The sole farmer with an ox may be able to feed his family, but the farmer with the motorized, mechanized industrial plow can feed an entire population. This analogy applies to thousands of other elements that make up our advanced western cultures, too.

Yes, oil is important, and anyone who lived in Holland in the 1970s, as I did, will recall "driverless Sundays" when an entire nation didn't drive a private automobile on Sunday for what I remember as at least a year, due to an Arab oil embargo. At that time, the industrialized west was totally dependent on Arab oil, and on OPEC (the Organization of the Petroleum Exporting Countries).

But, times and technology have both changed and solutions to our problems here in the United States are needed. Our simple solution here is to just pack up our bags and go home. That's it. Let's bring everyone home and concentrate on our own problems. We need to exit slowly, of course, strategically and gracefully, but it is no longer in our economic interest to remain there. Do we need to protect ourselves? Of course. We definitely need to keep vigilant watch with regard to our safety, and to take swift measures when our country is threatened.

The United States became the leading oil producing nation in the world in 2014.

Due to fracking, the United States became the leading oil producing nation in the world in 2014. And, we are slowly developing alternative energy strategies, such as wind and solar. These initiatives are not moving all that fast yet, but they are moving and as time goes on, more and more people will convert to them. This means that we will need less oil, and that our country can survive and thrive on what we produce here at home.

It is undeniable that we have urgent problems here that demand our full attention. Homelessness, education, immigration, taxes, jobs, and everything else we've discussed here all need vast amounts of attention from our best and brightest leaders. We are not going to solve a thousand or more years of fighting in the Middle East in our lifetime. It's just not going to happen. So let's leave them to it and get on with taking care of our own.

AMERICA'S SIMPLE SOLUTIONS

The history of the Middle East area is ancient and complex, and we just don't need to get involved. Let's simply stay home and take care of our own problems.

That said, we definitely need to keep vigilant watch with regard to our safety, and take swift measures when our country is threatened, but that doesn't mean conducting a trillion dollar ground war in a country where we are not wanted.

18

What Other Countries Do Right

SO FAR, WE'VE LOOKED AT MANY CONCERNS issue-by-issue, and learned how other countries handle these concerns. Let's now shoot from the hip and look at it all a different way. Rather than issue-by-issue, let's take a quick run-down country-by-country, to get a different look at what each country is doing right.

Looking at the way other countries handle issues is an excellent opportunity to get a feel for where the country is headed as a whole, as compared to the United States. It is also an opportunity for us to modify their success, and make it work for us, too. This is not a complete list, and is not intended to be, but you will be able to see how some other countries are moving forward.

Australia and New Zealand

These countries practice a "rule of law." This is the idea that law should govern a nation—as opposed to being governed by arbitrary decisions of government officials. In a rule of law, no one is above the law, and penalties for all are clear cut. This takes some of the hit-or-miss concept out of the courtroom and saves taxpayers money. We, too, live in a rule of law in America, but our judicial system has more leeway here in imposing sentences and penalties than in other countries.

A rule of law brings order, and people in Australia and New Zealand have turned that sense of order into a relaxed and focused business atmosphere. Australia, in particular, is a good place to invest. Their economy has slowed some recently, but the job market is holding and people have saved well there. We here in the US tend to spend more than we have, then find we have nothing to fall back on in an emergency. Saving, and living within our means, will bring comfort and security to all US families.

Canada

Canada is our close and friendly neighbor to the north, and they are absolutely rocking it on the health care front. They spend less per person than we do, and *everyone* is covered. Many families in the United States still cannot afford healthcare, or the deductibles. Some call Canada's system socialized medicine. I don't care what it is called, it works and we should adapt the idea for our own country. Keeping citizens healthy also keeps them productive, and productivity leads to a strong economy, so this issue is a very important one.

China

We don't need to imitate China in most things, but their brand of capitalism works, and their growth rate sure beats ours. Plus, more freedoms and lower taxes allow their economy to work better than ours. China (and many other Asian countries) are also eclipsing us in the area of technology. We must educate our best and brightest, then put them to work solving our current and future problems. We cannot be competitive, much less a global leader, unless we can keep up with other countries.

France

France has a lot of problems, but I would much rather be sick in France than in the US. The costs are much, much lower. We must get our costs of health care under control, while still delivering quality service. France has done this, as have many other countries

Plus, some doctors in France still make house calls. Whoever decided it was a good idea for a sick person to go out into the world, and spread germs all over the place while they slowly traipsed their way to their doctor's office so they could be around a whole lot of other sick people? Would it not be better for people who are very, very ill to stay in bed and let the doctor come to them?

With as much modern technology as we have, everything from lab tests to x-rays can be done on site and in the home. Of course France has doctor's offices, too, and people do go them regularly, but only a miniscule number of doctors in the United States make house calls. Our current insurance companies do not allow it. We need to control our legion of malpractice and accident lawyers, and impose stiff penalties for filing frivolous law suits that tie up our legal system.

Germany

The German people, as a whole, are frugal, hard working, and diligent. This all adds up to great productivity and a strong sense of pride in a job well done. That pride extends to their entire nation. We have too many people here in the United States who are pulling against each other. As individuals, let's task ourselves to do a better job and be proud of what we do. The extended benefits will then spread throughout entire companies and provide happier workplaces. I've also found that if you are happy at work, you are also happier in your personal life.

Hong Kong

Hong Kong has a 16 percent flat tax that from time to time delivers surplus money back into the hands of the people. Isn't that cool? With that system in place, we'd have no more incomprehensible tax laws. We spend so much time, frustration, and money navigating our current tax system, and even then two different families of the same size, making the same amount of money, and living next door to each other would pay a completely different amount of tax.

India

India actually is a country that is *overly* democratic. Everyone has a voice. They have too many regulations, but have quite good growth in spite of it. Their citizens value knowledge, and are highly educated in science, math, engineering, and physics. We cannot let students from other countries continue to outshine our own. Yes, we have many families who place high importance on education, but not enough. We Americans are bright people, so let's tap into all that possibility.

Italy

Italy is highly taxed, but the importance of family is very strong. This allows family members to pull together better than Americans do when the going gets rough. Then rather than the demeaning government support that we have, they have nurturing, and powerful family support.

In addition, lots of friendly smiles and excellent food throughout the country brings about a huge tourist industry. Tourism means dollars and a boost to the economy. With the exception of some of our Southern cities, we have a lot to learn about hospitality. We could, and should look to Italy in this area.

Israel

Israel supports its technology sector far more than we do. We've discussed the importance of this before, but it is important enough to mention again. In addition to training our young people in this area, we must support technology businesses who will develop applications and technologies that will lead us into our future.

Japan

This is a nation filled with debt, but they are still the number three economy in the world. Japan is also a huge tourist destination for Chinese tourists, because the Japanese consumer market is so highly developed. We can do better in tourism, which brings in huge dollars and could deliver a nice little economic jump start to some areas of our country.

Scandinavia

I am grouping all the Nordic countries, Finland, Norway, and Sweden, to-gether because, they are all doing most of the same things right. One of those things is religious tolerance. People in those countries, for the most part, are spiritual but not fanatic about their religion. My feeling is that our Republican party has not won elections in recent years because they are not following the vision of the Founding Fathers—they are too concerned about religion. Remember that not all of our Founding Fathers were Chris-tians, and some were deists or even atheists. The Scandinavian countries are also very close to closing the gender and equality gap, and most other countries around the world are far ahead of us in this area, as well.

Singapore

As with China, in the economic sphere in Singapore there is more capital-ism and individual freedom. As a result, their standard of living has in-creased ten times over the past few decades, so let's elect people who will look at the successes of countries such as Singapore, and will lead us into similar success. The Singapore government supports business, the Amer-ican government does not and the growth results speak for themselves.

Switzerland

Back to health care. Major heart surgery here in the United States can cost a half million dollars. In Switzerland, in the best heart clinics in the world, major heart surgery is right at fifty thousand dollars. Let's get our health-care costs down, and let's make it a priority. Welfare in Switzerland is de-signed to get people off the system and to lend a helping hand only for a limited time of need. It is not a system that is easily abused, and it allows an abuser of the system to be a professional welfare lifelong recipient. Let's study what Switzerland does and apply the lessons to our faulty American system.

Thailand

Like Italian citizens, the people of Thailand are full of smiles. These gentle people also have a lot of excellent good food, and they are very open to other cultures. In the United States, we have more cultures mixed together than any other country in the world. However, many of us are rigid and un-accepting of others histories and cultures. People from "bad neighborhoods" aside, it is both fun and interesting to learn how different people celebrate and live their lives.

United Kingdom

Out of all the no- or low-growth European countries, Britain is typically the leader in European growth. Yes, the Brits have spent centuries being industrious people, but (1970s aside) their long-standing success shows that free markets and capitalism still work best. We have followed their lead many times, but now it is time to dig deeper and pull out the minute details that have made them so strong for so long.

Uruguay

There is a lot of individual freedom in Uruguay, so it is an attractive country for many businesses and investors. While our current elected officials are swamping us with regulations, we have the ability to change that through the simple process of the vote. Until we can attract foreign business and investment, we will be in a stagnant pattern of growth. During recent Uruguay President José Mujica's five-year presidential term, Uruguay became a hot bed of economic policies that favor business and foreign investment. Uruguay has much to teach us on this front.

Vietnam

We spend about nine thousand dollars every year per person for healthcare, and our longevity is about seventy-eight years. Vietnam, on the other hand, spends just three *hundred* dollars a year per person and their longevity averages three years less than ours. Essentially, when we purchase a Rolls Royce, Vietnam purchases a Bentley for 3 percent of the cost. They keep costs down by being efficient in all that they do, while we are wasteful in our time and usage of goods. As individuals and as a society we can look to Vietnam and come away far more efficient in all that we do.

All Countries (except the United States)

Our last category is all of the countries in the world, except the United States, and it has to do with gun control. Just as we do with a driver's license, we must approach gun use with a safety first attitude. We must not give lethal weapons to kids, the mentally ill, and criminal felons. The US is different in their thoughts about gun control from virtually every other country in the rest of the world. We also have, by far, the highest incidences of gun killings in the civilized world. It must stop, and it must stop now. Let's look to five or six of our top allies, and see how they handle this issue. I know we can find a way to do this and still honor our second amendment.

We must not give lethal weapons to kids, the mentally ill, and criminal felons.

So where does this all put the United States? We need to make education our top national priority, and we need to become a business friendly nation with lower taxes. We have to stop incurring unpayable debt for future generations. We also must support real productive growth and stop printing paper money to create the illusion of growth. Then we need to tune into the new global world and welcome foreign business with a favorable business and tax environment. Once they invest in America and create jobs we must support them.

We must become a nation that requires background checks, and safety training for all gun purchases. And, we have to find ways to boost tourism, streamline our court system, lower health care and truly make it inclusive to everyone. Our young children have to be taught the importance of freedom, and they need better educations so they can develop new technology for the future. And, we all can start, right now, to take personal pride in our individual work. Most important, we need to love our and value our families every day.

We must become a nation that requires background checks, and safety training for all gun purchases.

We can make some of these changes in the voting booth and others by innovation and creativity. But, the important take away is that we *can* make them. We can make these simple changes that will make America greater than it already is. And, we can start today.

19

Choose Wisely

Remember, democracy never lasts long. It wastes, exhausts, and murders itself.
There was never a democracy yet that did not commit suicide.
—John Adams, Second President of the US, diplomat

The best guarantee against the abuse of power consists in the freedom,
the purity, and the frequency of popular elections.
—John Adams, Second President of the United States

MY OPINION? WHEN ONLY 8 PERCENT OF voters turn up for an election, it is disrespectful to our many fellow Americans who sacrificed their lives for our freedom. These brave people gave the ultimate sacrifice for our freedom to make changes in this country. Then, a majority of our citizens are not respectful enough of that sacrifice to cast a vote. That is very sad.

Understood, voting takes time out of a busy day. It takes a little more time to actually become informed about who to vote for. But, voting puts our local, state, and national leaders in place, leaders who shape the direction of our country. Voting is an important right.

Our children should also see their older generations undertaking the serious duty and responsibility of voting. The most important teaching a parent can do is to set a good example. An example is the greatest teaching tool a parent has, and if we don't teach our children the importance of voting our conscience now, in the future we will have an even lower voter turn out than we do now. Hard to believe there can be a lower number than 8 percent, but if our children do not learn about the importance of voting, it will happen. Our children must learn this, and learn to cherish it so they can prove wrong John Adams's admonition that "Democracy never lasts long."

Benjamin Franklin once said, "any fool can criticize and complain and most fools do." Then in his autobiography, *An American Life*, Ronald Reagan said, "If you don't vote, you are part of the problem and you don't have the right to squawk." Both of these statements are true, but which one best describes you?

The objective of this book was to give a global perspective, not to criticize but to inform readers about what is going on in the rest of the world. It was written to show how we Americans are doing relative to other countries that are facing many of the same dilemmas. My goal was to tell Americans what has worked well elsewhere, and what could work here in the United States.

In addition to the many issues we have discussed, including the importance of voting, there is also the very important issue of finding qualified leaders who understand our problems, truly understand them, and understand America's role in our new global society. It is hard for leaders to find a solution if they don't understand the problem.

So far, we have repeatedly elected politicians who have made us entitled to many things. At the very least, we should be given a list of all our entitlements, something that shows the full extent of our self-gifting, a list of everything we are "getting for free." These gifts are entitlements, and you may recall that not many entitlements exist in the thriving new economies of Asia.

If we had such a list of our entitlements, we could at least appreciate what the rest of American society is doing for us, and how this stacks up in comparison to the rest of the world. If we had such a list, it might help us realize that no one has the "right" to the long list of entitlements that we now receive. Unfortunately, our list of entitlements is so long and so convoluted, and many are buried so deeply within incomprehensible laws, that we'd never be able to come up with a complete list.

As a society, it is best that we earn some of our current entitlements ourselves. Either that, or someone else such as a spouse, parent, or guardian, needs to earn them and give them to us. This kind of self-reliance will create and restore great pride in our families and in ourselves. Do some people need some of our current entitlements? Absolutely. I have said this before, and it is also true that we will always have a few people who cannot help themselves. It is our duty as good citizens to help those who cannot help themselves. But, we should let people who *can* help themselves get on with it.

We must also decide as voting members of the United States if we want to allow the rest of the world to absorb our excess printed currency so we can live beyond our means. Shouldn't we instead seek out candidates who address this issue honestly, candidates who tell us who is paying for what, and what the consequences will be?

It is essential for Americans today to realize that the rest of the world is supporting us in living beyond our means. This living beyond our means is what is happening now, but it will not last forever. So let's seek out people who are talking about this in a public forum. Can't find anyone who is? Let's dig deeper to find excellent candidates. Maybe one of them will even be you.

It is essential for Americans today to realize that the rest of the world is supporting us in living beyond our means.

Remember what happened to the UK in the 1970s when its pound sterling was dethroned as the world's reserve currency? In October 2015 the International Monetary Fund (IMF) added the Remembi (the Chinese

Yuan) to their basket of currencies. This is so the rest of the world doesn't have to subsidize America living beyond its means forever. This party we've been living in will not go on too much longer, so our current reality will stop in a short period of time. If we look to Britain, we know what happens when a nation is forced to lower its standard of living. No growth and no productivity. Which current candidate in your area, or nationally, is telling us that we are on borrowed time?

I recognize the good intentions of economists who say all this doesn't make a difference because "we owe the money for the most part to ourselves." But the real world I travel in doesn't work the way their theory does. To use an example, people in Hong Kong work productively and create government surpluses with their efforts. The surplus monies are then returned to the citizens of Hong Kong. This is real. The same goes for sectors of the marketplace in India, Korea, and elsewhere in Asia. Countries grow wealthier through productivity.

Countries grow wealthier through productivity.

Maybe an economy could be jump-started temporarily through a short term "printing press fling." But as a long term strategy it's like saying the human body will thrive on a constant dose of chocolate cake, or that a person with a debt addiction will become solvent by acquiring and incurring more debt. That's just not real. Think carefully now. Who among your current crop of candidates have you heard addresses this issue?

Question current policy, and become informed. That is the rule of the day. When politicians promise, we need to ask how the promise will be paid for. There is no free lunch. There just isn't. Maybe there is some payment for a temporary, short period, but nothing is free. This is how the global economy works, not on Tinker Bell's magic wand economics. I don't care what anyone says, or has as a new-fangled scheme to create wealth out of thin air, it is all economic fiction, plain and simple. Is there a candidate who is honest, and tells you what you don't want to hear?

Let's reopen the discussion of our Founding Fathers to see how we are doing. If debt is skyrocketing at an unsustainable pace, we can't dismiss it. Our government can't always print more money. That strategy will eventually catch up with us. An inflated currency is simply that, a currency whose value is inflated and the currency will purchase less. So we can fool ourselves, but eventually that three-dollar loaf of bread will cost fifteen.

Voters need to question. Remember that James Madison said, "Not always will there be great leaders in power." The ballot box is a corrective means. We desperately need to use it.

When politicians promise, we need to ask how the promise will be paid for.

Remember, too, that our government is there to serve us, the people. It is not the other way around. An eternally growing government is absolutely unsustainable, and cannot continue. We all have heard examples of how wasteful our government is when it comes to purchases and use of our hard-earned dollars. We need candidates who, after being elected, will spend reasonable amounts of money for reasonable things. We need to hold our government and our elected officials accountable, and get on solid footing.

Remember that our government gives entitlements and pensions that private industry could never afford. We must end government salaries that are so high that they help put our cities, towns, states, and country in financial ruin. We also need to rescue people from what FDR correctly called the narcotic of welfare and limit open-ended welfare programs. We must motivate our population to work, and let people be productive for their own well-being, happiness, and satisfaction. Let's end this cycle of welfare dependency, which robs people of their dignity.

We need candidates who, after being elected, will spend reasonable amounts of money for reasonable things.

Let's also educate our children properly, and globally and competitively expand opportunity for everyone. We *can* meet the challenge of helping businesses expand productively and stop over-regulating them. Then, let's help the truly needy who cannot help themselves, and find candidates and elected officials who understand this, and will get this done. We need actions, not words.

Most of us agree that we desperately need tax reform. Let's make this happen so we can get behind business and create real growth. We need jobs, productive well paying jobs that create real wealth. We will then have real money and profits to reinvest, rather than more debt. Plus, our government will collect more revenue. This has been proven over and over. We must also attract higher levels of civil servants, and in the short term, get people from outside of government to temporarily devote time to identify and correct the mis-management our elected officials have created. Just like us, our government must live within its means. This means Congress must stop perpetual over-spending.

We need to return jurisdiction of local matters back to localities, and to the states, as the states originally created the federal government, not the other way around. If we are to survive as a country, we need to elect officials that share these objectives, and have a reasonable, workable plan to get it done.

> "We had strayed a great distance from our founding father's vision of America: they regarded the central government's responsibility as that of providing national security, protecting our democratic freedoms, and limiting the government's intrusion into our lives-in sum, the protection of life, liberty and the pursuit of happiness."
> —Ronald Reagan, 33rd governor of California (1967-1975), 40th president of the United States (1981-1989)

Yes, I've quoted Reagan a lot, but he was right. Our government *has* strayed far over its boundaries, and our good intentions allowed this to happen. We must reverse this trend. It won't happen overnight, but it will happen, because it must.

Let us also remember the many great and universal truths from other people, people such as Mandela, Ghandi, Churchill, Kennedy, Friedman and others like them. The human race has been down many of the roads we now face before, and we found solutions. We found practical solutions. How easily we forget from one generation to the next.

Today we are faced with the same set of problems that many countries before us have faced. The difference is that today we have information at our fingertips and the successful solutions that others have developed to turn into real answers. So, why do we struggle? Why do we say things are not as simple today? Life and societies have always been complex. Will the simple solutions we implement be immediately perfect? No, but we will get started, and progress will be made.

As a country, we need to become smart, globally smart. When we impose the highest corporate taxes in the world, along with a burdensome amount of regulation, we must also consider the position of an international investor who today can invest anywhere in the world. Would you invest and create jobs in an environment that is anti-business and highly taxed? The smart answer is, "No." Guess what? Other people feel the same way, and this is a part of America's decline. Each of us needs to tune into what's going on globally.

Let's also find a fair tax rate so US corporations won't leave money overseas. "A rising tide lifts all boats," said John F. Kennedy, so let's not get bogged down in meaningless words. Instead, let's implement something that works. Government doesn't create new industries and great new revolutionary inventions. Business does. So let's get behind the hopes and dreams of the next generation of entrepreneurs, and help them make all this happen. Let's not tax them to death so they have no capital to finance their fledgling business's growth. With the right mind-set, and the right people, we really can remove the umpteen thousand regulations that strangle the everyday activities of start ups and other businesses.

Does anyone care if a few dozen people like Bill Gates and Steve Jobs get multi-billionaire rich? We actually need another thousand people just like them. Between Apple and Microsoft, just look at what they've done. These two men alone have actually changed the world. Dramatically. So let's get more companies like Microsoft and Apple, successful companies that employ tens of thousands of people, many of them highly paid.

Wouldn't you love to have excellent public education for our children, full employment, a brand spanking new infrastructure, and cities that don't go bankrupt—all because the industries in these cities are buzzing with activity? To make that happen, you have to vote. Your friends, family, neighbors, and co-workers also have to vote. Even if we all vote for what turns out to be the "wrong" candidate, an essential element of success is failure. We'll get it right eventually, but we need to get started. Too many Americans have abandoned the process. This is not okay. Our freedoms have to be respected and voting is an important one. Every of us can make a difference and we need to do our very important and essential part inside the voting booth.

Every of us can make a difference and we need to do our very important and essential part inside the voting booth.

If you can't find a candidate you can believe in, consider running yourself. If you are passionate about affecting positive change and have a great plan for making it happen, then run. At the very least, get involved in the local decision making process in your town or county. Attend a planning commission, school board, or city council meeting to see what is going on. If you are so inclined, maybe you'll even agree to serve on a committee, or volunteer to lead a clean-up project at a park in your town. Get involved.

You must, because you matter. Your opinion matters, because you are an American. You are one of the many millions who make up our great nation, and I say those words "great nation" with pride, because America is still great in many ways. Together, however, we can all make it much, much better—and stop our decline.

We can do that through the voting process that our Founding Fathers set up for us, by getting involved, by caring enough to do something constructive that will benefit our country. You can make a difference, especially with your vote.

It is human nature to complain, even when things are going well, but as I leave you to ponder the future of the United States of America, I'd like you to keep in mind one more quote. This one is from Mahatma Ghandi, the leader of the independence movement in British-ruled India: "Be the change you wish to see in the world."

"Be the change you wish to see in the world."

Be the change. As you have seen, one person, one vote, can make a difference. Be that voice. Be that vote. Then enlist everyone you can think of to join you in casting their votes to make the changes that our country needs. Together, these votes will start to turn the tide and soon, America will once again be the nation that our Founding Fathers envisioned.

Vote your conscience. Vote your heart. It is a very simple solution.

THE END

Acknowledgements

Dreams are a preview of what transpires in your life. Last year, when my guts were churning as I watched the United States go through some growing pains (and never being one to sit silently on the sidelines), I dreamed of writing a book. Some of the things that seemed to be going wrong here in America I didn't see as a problem elsewhere, or it was a problem that had already been fixed. During a lunch last year, a dear friend listened to my observations and said, "You should write a book." I answered that was exactly my plan.

He immediately took out his phone and made a call. "Neville," he said. "I have someone here you need to talk to." Long story short, thanks big time to Neville and Cindy Johnson of Cool Titles for believing in my literary dreams, and giving a first time author a chance to share a hardearned global vision that was formed over a lifetime . . . and millions of miles of travel.

Thanks must also go to David Ostrove, California Attorney, California Certified Public Accountant and Certified Specialist in Taxation Law for his review of pertinent areas of the manuscript.

A very special thank you to Lisa Wysocky for assisting me in writing the book. This book would never have happened without Lisa's talent, keen insights, her patience, and optimism, and her "buttery" literary skills. My four-year-old Iggy calls her his dada's "Mona Lisa," and Iggy was right. Now I do too.

Lastly, much gratitude to my gorgeous wife, Amanda Shi Werts, for patiently watching me night after night research the materials for this book, and tolerating the days and weeks I sat in front of my computer and wasn't with the family. I also give her a deep expression of gratitude for her guidance and explanations of Chinese and other Asian cultures (which we visited together), and her very practical down-to-earth insights about what the emerging powerhouse called China is doing well, and what China is struggling with. Amanda shared with me various Chinese proverbs and elements of the Mandarin language, which gave me a much better understanding of what really was going on in Chinese society. No westerner can truly understand China by being on the outside looking in. Thanks, wifey!

Appendix A: Chapter Summaries

Chapter 1—The New Global World: A Conversation in Beijing

Individuals can make an enormous impact. Indeed they do—and always have throughout history. Remember that each of us is an individual who can make a difference.

Chapter 2—The Founding Fathers

We all have an obligation to help, assist, and support the truly needy. We have zero obligation to assist those who abuse our welfare system. In fact, we have an obligation to vote for those who will eliminate abuse, and eliminate those elected officials who abuse our compassionate generosity. The truly needy could be in the area of 10 percent of our population, depending on time and circumstance, and include the elderly, handicapped, perpetually ill, orphaned youth, and disabled veterans, among others. The truly needy do not include the able bodied who abuse and profit from our welfare system. Also, question facts presented by the government, as government propaganda is not limited to totalitarian states.

Chapter 3—Freedom and Democracy

Individual freedom and wealth creation go hand in hand, and nations that allow citizens many freedoms usually become wealthy. Also, capitalism coupled with individual freedom and the use of the free market works—and is the most efficient system to create wealth. Central planning and socialistic policies don't produce the intended result, and don't work, and any system must be judged by actual results and not by the intention.

The good news: many of today's problems have already been answered brilliantly by our Founding Fathers and previous leaders of our nation. Let's teach the ideas of the Founding Fathers to the youth of America, so they can understand their ideas and wise counsel. Then, they can apply this wisdom to problems they will face as adults.

"Government is not the solution, government is the problem," and "The ten most dangerous words: I am from the government, I am here to help."
—Ronald Reagan

Chapter 4—Family

Work and family are the foundation of life, and the foundation of society. The Chinese hold the position of the family at the highest level, so America, take note of what makes up the success of modern societies on the rise. Plus, our American healthcare system is symptomatic of our priorities being out of sync. Let's adopt Canada's system tomorrow.

Chapter 5—Education

The most important element of investment in the infrastructure of a prosperous nation is the education of the present and next generations. Education is actually a "pass key" that opens almost every door that is currently closed to the youth of today and tomorrow.

Chapter 6—Healthcare

Let's adopt Canada's health system, or do a hybrid of their system. Americans must also be educated about nutrition as a means of preventative medicine, and this includes teaching our doctors about nutrition. We also need to appoint a private industry advisory board to study the healthcare success of other nations, and present viable proposals to our executive and legislative branches.

Chapter 7—Religion

To respect the memory of all who have worked for, fought for, and died for America, it is our obligation, and the duty of every American citizen, to vote and participate in each and every election.

Chapter 8—Immigration

America is a nation of immigrants, and our social security system would collapse within a number of years if we did not have new American immigrants to support it.

Chapter 9—Taxation

Man acts most efficiently when acting in his own self interest. Government, however, is a creator of wealth inequality through debt, debasement of the currency, and burdensome regulations that make it impossible for the little guy, or the young start up entrepreneur, to succeed. High taxes produce low revenues for the government, but lower taxes produce higher revenues for the government. Not initially, but it does happen once lower rates are in place and market forces have taken effect, as it stimulates overall growth.

"The more you take from the productive members of society, the less productive they become." —Porter Stansberry

America is not the world's policeman, nor its teacher or mentor. Instead, America can help other nations by taking care of its own internal needs and by becoming the shining light on the hill.

Chapter 10—Voting

In the mid and long term, you cannot get out of debt by incurring more debt. Get involved, vote your conscious, and encourage others to do so, as well.

Chapter 11—Environment

Climate change and pollution are two different subjects: the latter is about the negligence, stupidity and the greed of mankind; the former is something that has happened since the beginning of time. We need to understand the distinction, and recall that mankind is an important component of the world ecosystem.

Chapter 12—Welfare, Social Security, and Entitlements

Children are to be nurtured and cared for. Plus, entitlements are out of control and must be reduced. Originally, Americans were entitled to have honor, hard work, morality, personal integrity, respect of our fellow man, and a dedication to personal responsibility. These entitlements made our country the greatest hope for mankind, but no government can bestow these entitlements on you. Only you can. Unless you are among the small percentage of the truly needy, your well-being is your own responsibility. The goal of welfare should be to eliminate the need for welfare, not to perpetuate a welfare bureaucracy.

"The government has proven totally ineffective at dealing with poverty in America. The data is conclusive that government efforts are far more likely to be the cause of the wealth gap than the solution." —Porter Stansberry

Chapter 13—Gender and Equality

Gender makes no difference. Equal pay for whomever can do the job. Equal benefits as well. It's that simple.

Chapter 14—Business and Commerce

It is common sense to look to solutions of other countries that have successfully implemented the ideas, and to learn from their success as well as their failures.

The Chinese Remembi (Yuan) will soon assume a dominate role as one of the most important world's reserve currencies, more important even than the Euro, Yen, pound sterling, or Swiss franc. And, it will absolutely rival the dollar. The ascent of the Yuan will surprise America and force the US to curtail printing dollars, which will reduce the standard of living of the average American.

Asia is also adapting the successful policies that brought the western world to financial preeminence. In contrast, the western world is adapting the failed economic policies and burdensome regulations that Asia, China, Russia, and numerous other countries are in the process of abandoning.

We must remember that government exists for and is empowered by the people. This is why everyone has an obligation to vote.

Chapter 15—Technology

The world today is global. Jump on board and don't get left behind. Also, costs of the civil judicial system today are so high that justice only exists for those who can afford it. This is another form of wealth inequality created by the government. It is imperative that we the people demand the liberty of the individual and control our government, and maintain our individual freedom as outlined by the Founding Fathers.

Chapter 16—Crime and Gun Control

There are ways to honor the second amendment and also bring sanity to gun ownership. Safety training must be an essential requirement to owning a gun. And, these safety norms must be controlled by states and localities.

Chapter 17—Oil and the Middle East

Flat tax coupled with a consumption tax is the only fair taxation system and will stimulate overall growth. It also gives the taxed a true feeling of participation, ownership in the society, and dignity. Remember, too, it is smart to avoid walking in bad neighborhoods.

Chapter 18—What Other Countries Do Right

The decline of the west and America can only be reversed by people who understand the problem—and demand a solution. Let's look to the successes in other countries and modify their systems to fit our needs.

Chapter 19—Choose Wisely

Governments produce and create nothing. A government is not a wealth creator, but it is in the business of wealth redistribution. When you create nothing, the only way you can redistribute wealth is to take it from someone else. Government in America today sucks capital out of the productive private economy sector and uses it for activities in the public sector.

Appendix B: Resources

Following are a few interesting nonpartisan resources that I encountered in my fact-finding process for this book that might make you think about what is going on here in America. If, after perusing them, I hope you will vote your conscience in every election, and call your legislators to make your opinion known.

Disabilities and Welfare

https://www.census.gov/newsroom/releases/archives/miscellaneous/cb12-134.html

https://www.census.gov/newsroom/press-releases/2015/cb15-97.html

http://www.usatoday.com/story/money/personalfinance/2015/01/17/cheat-sheet-states-with-most-food-stamps/21877399/

http://www.usatoday.com/story/money/personalfinance/2015/01/17/cheat-sheet-states-with-most-food-stamps/21877399/

Economy

http://www.wsj.com/articles/u-s-gdp-expands-at-0-2-pace-in-first-quarter-1430310699

http://www.nytimes.com/1990/01/17/opinion/the-reagan-boom-greatest-ever.html

Education

https://nces.ed.gov/fastfacts/display.asp?id=4

http://www.iie.org/Research-and-Publications/Open-Doors

https://nces.ed.gov/surveys/pisa/

http://www.cnn.com/2012/05/31/opinion/bennett-china-us-schools/

https://www.studentsfirst.org/pages/the-stats

http://monitor.icef.com/2015/05/chinese-enrolment-in-the-us-shifting-increasingly-to-undergraduate-studies/

Environment

http://news.nationalgeographic.com/news/2014/08/140818-elephants-africa-poaching-cites-census/

http://designtoimprovelife.dk/index-award-2015-winners-talks/
http://www.worldwildlife.org/habitats/forest-habitat
http://www.cnbc.com/2014/12/18/china-makes-pollution-3m-makes-products-to-help-them-with-it.html
http://www.cnbc.com/2015/08/18/china-air-pollution-far-worse-than-thought-study.html
https://www.rt.com/usa/311794-oklahoma-earthquake-fracking-blamed/
http://www.cnbc.com/2015/06/19/quakes-not-caused-by-fracking-but-by-water-disposal-study.html
http://www.usatoday.com/story/money/business/2014/09/15/faulty-gas-well-pollute-water/15631955/

Families

https://www.census.gov/prod/2013pubs/p20-570.pdf
http://www.washingtonpost.com/blogs/she-the-people/wp/2014/06/23/global-view-how-u-s-policies-to-help-working-families-rank-in-the-world/
http://abcnews.go.com/Business/us-industrialized-nation-paid-maternity-leave/story?id=30852419
http://www.huffingtonpost.com/2014/06/23/white-house-working-parents-policies_n_5518197.html

Freedom

The Third Wave: Democratization in the Late Twentieth Century by Samuel P. Huntington

Founding Fathers

http://www.Foundingfathersquotes.com

Gender and Equality

http://www.mspb.gov/netsearch/viewdocs.aspx?docnumber=606214&version=608056&application=ACROBAT
https://www.opm.gov/policy-data-oversight/data-analysis-documentation/federal-employment-reports/reports-publications/executive-branch-employment-by-gender-and-racenational-origin/

http://www.americasjobexchange.com/career-advice/women-and-equality
http://www.pewresearch.org/fact-tank/2015/04/14/on-equal-pay-day-
everything-you-need-to-know-about-the-gender-pay-gap/
http://fortune.com/2014/10/27/best-countries-for-women/
http://reports.weforum.org/global-gender-gap-report-2014/rankings/

Gun Control

http://www.bradycampaign.org/about-gun-violence

Immigration

http://www.pewresearch.org/fact-tank/2015/07/24/5-facts-about-illegal-
immigration-in-the-u-s/
http://money.cnn.com/2014/11/20/news/economy/immigration-myths/
http://www.thedailybeast.com/articles/2014/09/18/careful-what-you-
wish-for-here-s-what-california-would-look-like-without-illegal-immi-
grants.html

Religion

http://blogs.reuters.com/faithworld/2013/12/03/dutch-bishops-give-
pope-francis-a-bleak-picture-of-catholic-church-in-decline/
http://www.cbs.nl/en-GB/menu/themas/vrije-tijd-cultuur/publicaties/ar-
tikelen/archief/2008/2008-2476-wm.htm

Taxes

http://investinholland.com/incentives-and-taxes/
http://www.ey.com/Publication/vwLUAssets/EY-Hong-Kong-2015-16-
Budget-Tax-Facts-en/$FILE/EY-Hong-Kong-2015-16-Budget-Tax-Facts-
en.pdf
http://www.taxpolicycenter.org/briefing-book/key-
elements/business/statutory.cfm

Technology

https://www.washingtonpost.com/news/wonk/wp/2014/10/02/4-4-bil-
lion-people-around-the-world-still-dont-have-internet-heres-where-they-
live/

http://www.theatlantic.co m/education/archive/2014/12/what-happens-when-kids-dont-have-internet-at-home/383680/

Voting
http://www.ISideWith.com

http://mentalfloss.com/article/59873/10-elections-decided-one-vote-or-less

http://abcnews.go.com/blogs/politics/2012/01/small-margins-a-look-back-at-the-closest-votes/

Wealth and Prosperity
http://www.prosperity.com

https://lif.blob.core.windows.net/lif/docs/default-source/publica-tions/2015-legatum-prosperity-index-pdf.pdf?sfvrsn=2 http://media.pros-perity.com/2014/pdf/publications/PI2014Brochure_WEB.pdf

Appendix C: Signers of the Declaration of Independence

Name	State	DOB	Birthplace	Age at Signing
Adams, John	MA	10/30/1735	Quincy, MA	40
Adams, Samuel	MA	9/27/1722	Boston, MA	53
Bartlett, Josiah	NH	11/21/1729	Amesbury, MA	46
Braxton, Carter	VA	9/10/1736	Newington, VA	39
Carroll, Charles	MD	9/19/1737	Annapolis, MD	38
Chase, Samuel	MD	4/17/1741	Somerset Co., MD	35
Clark, Abraham	NJ	2/15/1726	Elizabethtown, NJ	50
Clymer, George	PA	3/16/1739	Philadelphia, PA	37
Ellery, William	RI	12/22/1727	Newport, RI	48
Floyd, William	NJ	12/17/1734	Brookhaven, NY	41
Franklin, Benjamin	PA	1/17/1706	Boston, MA	70
Gerry, Elbridge	MA	7/17/1744	Marblehead, MA	32
Gwinnett, Button	GA	c. 1735	Gloucester, England	41
Hall, Lyman	GA	4/12/1724	Wallingford, CT	52
Hancock, John	MA	1/12/1737	Quincy, MA	40
Harrison, Benjamin	VA	4/7/1726	Charles City Co., VA	50
Hart, John	NJ	c. 1711	Hunterdon Co, NJ	65
Hewes, Joseph	NC	1/23/1730	Kingston, NJ	46
Heyward Jr., Thomas	SC	7/28/1746	St. Helena Parish, SC	30
Hooper, William	NC	6/17/1742	Boston, MA	34
Hopkins, Stephen	RI	3/7/1707	Providence, RI	69
Hopkinson, Francis	NJ	10/2/1737	Philadelphia, PA	38
Huntington, Samuel	CT	7/3/1731	Windham, CT	45
Jefferson, Thomas	VA	4/13/1743	Albemarle Co, VA	33
Lee, Francis Lightfoot	VA	10/14/1734	Mt. Pleasant, VA	41
Lee, Richard Henry	VA	1/20/1732	Stratford, VA	44
Lewis, Francis	NY	3/21/1713	Llandaff, Wales	63
Livingston, Philip	NY	1/15/1716	Albany, NY	60
Lynch Jr., Thomas	SC	8/5/1749	Prince George's Parrish, SC	26
McKean, Thomas	DE	3/19/1735	Chester Co., PA	42
Middleton, Arthur	SC	6/26/1742	Charleston, SC	34
Morris, Lewis	NY	4/8/1726	West Chester Co., NY	50
Morris, Robert	PA	1/31/1734	Liverpool, England	42

Occupation	#Marriages	#Children	DOD	Age at Death
Lawyer	1	5	7/4/1826	90
Merchant	2	2	10/2/1803	81
Physician	1	12	5/19/1795	65
Plantation	2	18	10/10/1797	61
Merchant, Plantation	1	7	11/14/1832	95
Lawyer	2	4	6/19/1811	70
Lawyer, Surveyor	1	10	9/15/1794	68
Merchant	1	8	1/24/1813	73
Lawyer, Merchant	2	16	2/15/1820	92
Land Speculator	2	3	8/4/1821	86
Scientist, Printer	1	3	4/17/1790	84
Merchant	1	7	11/23/1814	70
Merchant, Plantation	1	3	5/15/1777	42
Physician, Minister	2	1	10/19/1790	66
Merchant	1	2	10/8/1793	56
Plantation, Farmer	1	7	4/24/1791	65
Land owner	1	13	5/11/1779	68
Merchant	-	-	10/10/1779	49
Lawyer, Plantation	2	8	3/6/1809	62
Lawyer	1	3	10/14/1790	48
Merchant	2	7	4/13/1785	78
Lawyer, Musician	1	5	5/9/1791	53
Lawyer	1	2	1/5/1796	64
Lawyer, Plantation, Scientist	1	6	7/4/1826	83
Plantation	1	0	1/11/1797	62
Plantation, Merchant	2	6	6/19/1794	62
Merchant	1	7	12/30/1802	89
Merchant	1	9	6/12/1778	62
Lawyer	1	0	c. 1779	30
Lawyer	2	11	6/24/1817	83
Plantation	1	9	1/1/1787	44
Plantation	1	10	1/22/1798	71
Merchant, Land Speculator	1	7	5/8/1806	72

Name	State	DOB	Birthplace	Age at Signing
Morton, John	PA	c.1724	Ridley Township, PA	52
Nelson Jr., Thomas	VA	12/26/1738	Yorktown, VA	37
Paca, William	MD	10/31/1740	Abington, MD	35
Paine, Robert Treat	MA	3/11/1731	Boston, MA	45
Penn, John	NC	5/6/1740	Carolina Co, VA	36
Read, George	DE	9/18/1733	Northeast MD	42
Rodney, Caesar.	DE	10/7/1728	Dover, DE	47
Ross, George	PA	5/10/1730	New Castle, DE	46
Rush, Benjamin Dr.	PA	1/4/1746	Philadelphia, PA	30
Rutledge, Edward	SC	11/23/1749	Christ Church Parish, SC	26
Sherman, Roger	CT	4/19/1721	Newton, MA	55
Smith, James	PA	c. 1719	Northern Ireland	57
Stockton, Richard	NJ	10/1/1730	Princeton, NJ	45
Stone, Thomas	MD	c.1743	Charles Co., MD	33
Taylor, George	PA	c. 1716	Ireland	60
Thornton, Matthew	NH	c. 1714	Ireland	62
Walton, George	GA	c. 1741	Cumberland Co, VA	35
Whipple, William	NH	1/14/1730	Kittery, ME	46
Williams, William	CT	4/18/1731	Lebannon, CT	45
Wilson, James	PA	9/14/1742	Carskerdo, Scotland	33
Witherspoon, John	NJ	2/5/1723	Gifford, Scotland	53
Wolcott, Oliver	CT	11/20/1726	Windsor, CT	49
Wythe, George	VA	c. 1726	Elizabeth City Co, VA	50

Occupation	#Marriages	#Children	DOD	Age at Death
Farmer	1	8	c. 1777	53
Merchant, Plantation	1	13	1/4/1789	50
Lawyer, Plantation	2	5	10/13/1799	58
Lawyer, Scientist	1	8	5/12/1814	83
Lawyer	1	3	9/14/1788	48
Lawyer	1	5	9/21/1798	65
Plantation, Military	0	0	6/29/1784	55
Lawyer	1	3	7/14/1779	49
Physician	1	13	4/19/1813	67
Lawyer, Plantation	2	3	1/23/1800	50
Lawyer	2	15	7/23/1793	72
Lawyer	1	5	7/11/1806	87
Lawyer	1	6	2/28/1781	50
Lawyer	1	3	10/5/1787	44
Merchant	1	2	2/23/1781	65
Physician	1	5	6/24/1803	89
Lawyer	1	2	2/2/1804	63
Merchant	1	0	11/28/1785	55
Merchant	1	3	8/2/1811	80
Lawyer?	2	7	8/21/1798	55
Minister	2	12	11/15/1794	71
Lawyer	1	4	12/1/1797	71
Lawyer	2	1	6/8/1806	80

Book Club Questions

1. In general, do you agree with Mark's simple solutions? Why or why not?

2. What idea in this book do you disagree with most? Why?

3. Will you vote in your next township, city, county, state, or national election? Why or why not?

4. Have you ever felt that your vote or opinion doesn't count? If so, has that changed since reading this book?

5. Where do *you* feel America is headed?

6. What can you personally do to help our country?

7. After reading this book, have your political views changed ? If so, how?

8. Has reading this book made you want to visit any other countries? If so, which ones and why?

9. What made you pick up this book?

10. Before reading this book, had you been so aware of our Founding Fathers' or their views?

11. If you could set one action goal for yourself that would bring positive change you your family, what would it be?

12. What one piece of information that you learned in this book is most important to you, and why?

About the Author

Mark Werts is an entrepreneur, world traveler, and regular speaker at the University of Southern California (at the Roski School of Fine Arts and the Marshall School of Business) and at various business forums around the world. He is fluent in five languages, proficient in four more, and criss-crosses the globe in support of American Rag Cie., where he is Founder and CEO. When not traveling for business, he reads, spends time with his family, and can often be found on the nearest golf course. Find him online at:

MarkIWerts.com
Facebook.com/markiwerts
Twitter: @MarkIWerts

Index

The John Wooden Pyramid of Success

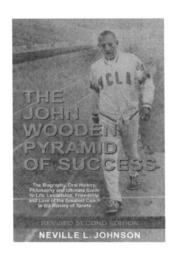

John Wooden, owner of many unequaled and mostly unapproachable records, coached the legendary UCLA basketball teams to ten national championships between 1963 and 1975. His accomplishments on the court alone make him a fascinating person. But Coach Wooden is much more: a philosopher and creator of the Pyramid of Success, which is a plain-spoken guide to achieving success that is packed with good, honest common sense. In this authorized biography, you will find the wisdom of this extraordinary man. Wooden allowed rare access to members of his family--brothers, children, and grandchildren who for the first time take you into his home life--as well as superstar athletes (Kareem Abdul-Jabbar, Bill Walton, Willie Naulls, Walt Hazzard, Gail Goodrich, Sidney Wicks plus many others) as well as nationally known broadcasters.

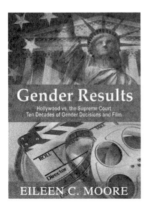

Gender Results

Eileen Moore, a Justice on the California Court of Appeal and author of the award-winning *Race Results*, presents a fresh comparison on gender biases that women face in film and within the US Supreme Court. From early stirrings of women's rights in 1848 in Seneca Falls, New York; through the pioneers of female equality, Moore delves into gender as no other author has before. Did movies foster the rights of women, or keep them harnessed to outdated roles? What about our legal system? How did our Supreme Court break the hearts of women, and then protect them? From workplace equality to women's rights, film and our legal system combined to both help and hinder American women.

Race Results

Eileen Moore, a justice on the California Appellate Court, brings a decade-by-decade comparison of Hollywood films and Supreme Court decisions, with regard to race. Beginning with *The Birth of a Nation* in 1915 and continuing through the new millennium, a surprising fact is that the United States Supreme Court, often perceived as out-of-touch and stuffy, is often more fair and liberal in their treatment of blacks than is Hollywood. Offset beautifully by more than twenty black and white photos, this in-depth study is sometimes shocking, often surprising, and a must-read for anyone interested in the history of film, law, race relations, pop culture . . . even our country.

Woodenisms

John Wooden was arguably the greatest coach, the greatest leader, of all time. These Woodenisms, a collection of his wisdom and sayings, will inspire, motivate, and prepare you for any challenge you face. Woodensims provide good common sense, and will assist you in being a leader and a team player, and will also give you strength to carry on in whatever you do. Excellent gift book, or source of daily motivation.